D1180063

Twayne's English Authors Series

Sylvia E. Bowman, *Editor*

INDIANA UNIVERSITY

Ronald Firbank

TEAS 93

Ronald Firbank

By JAMES DOUGLAS MERRITT

Brooklyn College, City University of New York

Twayne Publishers, Inc.   ::   New York

Preface

THIS book has the single purpose of introducing Ronald Firbank's work to a wider audience. It attempts to show that he was, initially, a writer in the *fin de siècle* or Decadent tradition who modified and eventually reshaped that tradition into thoroughly original novels and stories. It is not possible to "place" Firbank in a literary context because his work is unique; but it *is* possible to see that other writers, such as Evelyn Waugh, Ivy Compton-Burnett, and Norman Douglas, derived inspiration from him.

Firbank's chief novels are dealt with more or less chronologically, for the simple and obvious reason that one may clearly see how they move away from imitating a previous tradition and toward a new kind of literature. In Chapter I, the novel *Inclinations* is treated rather than in Chapter II, where chronologically it belongs, because it is unlike the important novels written between 1914 and 1921 with which that chapter deals. Chapter V deals with a collection of fragments and a play which were written over a period of more than thirty years; the reason for this is that the material is fragmentary and, therefore, should not be discussed in connection with the completed works discussed in the other chapters. Chapter V also contains a discussion of Firbank's only complete play which would be out of place in chapters dealing with the novels. All of the material dealt with in Chapter V has been published in a single volume entitled *The New Rythum and Other Pieces*, while all of the novels dealt with in the other chapters of this book have been published in a single volume entitled *The Complete Ronald Firbank*. A reader may use this book in conjunction with those two volumes and find that its structure is such that, as he progresses through Firbank's work, the chapters will nearly coincide.

Almost no attempt has been made to provide a thorough biography of Firbank for a number of reasons. The materials available are limited, and the myth which surrounds Firbank could very easily mislead one in forming an impression of him as a writer. His life was publicly frivolous, but his writing was a serious private matter. Biographical information is therefore limited to only the most interesting and significant details which appear to have a bearing on Firbank's writing. For those biographical details which I have included, I have depended almost entirely upon the information in I. K. Fletcher's *Memoir* of Firbank (which includes additional material by four other contemporaries) and Miriam J. Benkovitz's *A Bibliography of Ronald Firbank* (Soho Bibliographies [London, 1963]) which is a mine of information both bibliographical and biographical, and materials in the Berg Collection of the New York Public Library. Readers who desire more information about Firbank's private life are recommended to consult these books and materials.

I wish to express my debt to Dr. Robert Davis of the University of Oklahoma, who introduced me to Firbank and often made helpful suggestions. He is, of course, in no way responsible for any errors that may exist in this book. I am, in addition, grateful to New Directions and to Gerald Duckworth & Co., Ltd., for permission to quote from Firbank's works.

Contents

Chronology

1886   Ronald Firbank born in London on January 17. His full name was Arthur Annesley Ronald Firbank. The family home was at 40 Clarges St., off Piccadilly in the fashionable West End.

1896   During the first ten years of his life, Ronald is much doted on by his mother, and the family life is a pleasant one. Ronald is "delicate" in health. He enters, as a "special student," the Mortimer Vicarage School in Eton, Buckinghamshire. He is already writing and completes a "novel," *Lila*, which is unpublished.

1898   Firbank writes *Lady Appledore's Mesalliance*.

1900   Firbank enters Uppingham, a public school, in December.

1901   Firbank leaves Uppingham in April, and for two months studies with a private tutor. In September he goes to France to study languages and literature at Howley Grange, Sainte-Tulle, Basses-Alpes. Here he reads French literature which makes a great impression upon him. He has been writing plays which are unpublished except in fragments.

1902   Ronald's father is knighted.

1903   Firbank goes to St. Symphorien, Indre et Loire, to polish his French with a view toward entering the diplomatic service.

1904   Firbank leaves St. Symphorien in October; goes to live in Paris where he meets, according to some of his later Cambridge acquaintances, many of the fashionable literary and theater people of the period. His first publication appears in *Les Essais;* it is "La Princess aus Soleils" which he had written in English and translated into French.

1905   Firbank publishes, at his own expense, a volume containing *Odette* and *A Study in Temperament*. A "Poem in Prose" entitled "Souvenir d'Automne" is published in the Supplement to *The King and His Army and Navy*. He is still under the influence of the French writers and the English Decadents. He reads Dowson and Verlaine, and collects first editions of these writers. He visits Madrid from the end of February until July 6th. After his return to London he "crams" for a university, visits Paris toward the end of the year, and finally goes to The Parsonage, Bielside, Aberdeenshire, to be tutored for Cambridge.

1906 Firbank enters Trinity Hall, Cambridge, in October after more tutoring and publishes " 'The Wavering Disciple' A Fantasia" in *The Granta*, an undergraduate publication. He decorates his rooms elaborately and actively creates the image of an "Aesthete" though Trinity Hall is, at that time, a college known for its athletic prowess. Firbank exercises "for his figure" but escapes "ragging."

1907 Firbank publishes "A Study in Opal" in *The Granta*. Sir Joseph Firbank has money problems.

1908 Firbank enters the Roman Catholic Church, according to one of his professors; but few of his contemporaries seem to be aware of it.

1909 Firbank leaves Cambridge after his fifth term with the distinction of having never taken any examination while there.

1910– Firbank thinks of going into the Vatican Service; is unsuc-
1915 cessful in obtaining an appointment. Sir Thomas dies in 1910 and there is some financial problem, though Ronald continues to lead a luxurious life. He is writing fairly regularly, but does not publish until 1915 when *Vainglory* appears in a handsome edition for which he has paid the costs. In 1914 he had retired to Oxford to avoid the omnipresent evidence of World War I; the beginning of his major writing period. He drops his first two names and is simply Ronald Firbank.

1916 *Inclinations* is completed and published in June; "slightly revised" version of *Odette* is republished in December.

1917 *Caprice* is published in November at a total cost to Firbank of £116, including an illustration by Augustus John. Firbank is inducted into the army; discharged after one day's service.

1919 Firbank leaves Oxford for London. He reads a chapter of *Valmouth* to a group of people including Osbert and Sacheverell Sitwell, Siegfried Sassoon and other "literary" people. *Valmouth* is published in December at a personal cost of £116 and with a drawing by Augustus John.

1920   Firbank publishes (at his own expense) his play, *The Princess Zoubaroff*, from which he hopes to make money; not produced during his lifetime. He visits North Africa where he begins *Santal*.

1921   *Santal* is published, again at his own expense, while he is at Versailles at work upon *The Flower Beneath the Foot*. Visits Switzerland.

1922   *The Flower Beneath the Foot* is completed at Florence. Firbank visits the West Indies in search of material.

1923   *The Flower Beneath the Foot* is published and costs Firbank £208; it has a "decoration" by C. R. W. Nevinson and portraits of Firbank by Wyndham Lewis and Augustus John. Carl Van Vechten, in America, writes admiringly of Firbank; arranges for the publication of a chapter of his new novel. Firbank visits Spain; begins work on *Concerning the Eccentricities of Cardinal Pirelli*.

1924   Ronald's mother, Lady Firbank dies, which causes him great grief. *Sorrow in Sunlight*, his West Indian novel, is renamed *Prancing Nigger* by Carl Van Vechten and published in America, for once at the publisher's expense. Firbank actually makes a little money from this book and talk is begun about the possibility of producing a uniform American edition of his work. He has a certain vogue in "smart" circles, but is still unknown enough for the gushing *New York Times* reviewer to refer to *Valmouth* (1919) as *Vermouth*. In November, *Prancing Nigger*, with its original title, is published in England, eight months after its appearance in the U.S.

1925   Firbank completes *Concerning the Eccentricities of Cardinal Pirelli* in Rome; revises *Vainglory* and *Inclinations*. Goes to Egypt; begins *The New Rythum* about New York.

1926   Firbank leaves Cairo for Rome; dies on May 26th in the Hotel Quirinale; buried in the Protestant Cemetery; body later removed to the Catholic Cemetery at San Lorenzo. *Concerning the Eccentricities of Cardinal Pirelli* is published in June; Firbank had already paid Grant Richards, the publisher, £155. The book should have appeared in 1925, but it was held up by Richards' financial problems.

1928 *The Works of Ronald Firbank,* first collected edition, published simultaneously in London and New York in five volumes. A "Biographical Memoir" by Osbert Sitwell is included. The *Works* not complete.

1929– The "Rainbow Edition" of Firbank's work published in
1930 eight volumes by Duckworth.

1934 *The Artificial Princess* published for the first time.

1935 *Extravaganzas,* containing *The Artificial Princess* and *Concerning the Eccentricities of Cardinal Pirelli,* published in November.

1938 Translations of two novels are published in Paris as *La Princesse Artificielle* and *Suivi de Mon Piaffeur Noir.*

1949– "Omnibus Edition" of two volumes entitled *Five Novels*
1950 and *Three Novels.*

1961 *The Complete Ronald Firbank* published by Duckworth in London and imported by New Directions in America. Penguin publishes in paperback *Valmouth, Prancing Nigger,* and *Cardinal Pirelli.*

1962 *The New Rythum and Other Pieces* by Duckworth and, again, imported by New Directions who also published at the end of October a paperback edition of *The Flower Beneath the Foot* and *Prancing Nigger.*

1965– Limited editions of two short pieces, *The Wind and the*
1966 *Roses* ('65) and *Far Away* ('66) published.

CHAPTER 1

"A St. Sebastian with Too Many Arrows"

I *Introduction*

RONALD FIRBANK is scarcely known to American readers of English novels, yet so eminent a critic as Edmund Wilson has called him "one of the finest English writers of his period" and added to that accolade the prediction that he was "one of those most likely to become a classic." [1] Since Firbank's period coincided with, in part, the period of Virginia Woolf and D. H. Lawrence, to name only two, Wilson's appraisal assumes added significance. And Wilson is far from being alone in his admiration. Firbank's comparative obscurity is the result of such diverse factors as the unavailability (until recently) of most of his work, and a legend that has grown up around him which makes him into a late-blooming "decadent" flower, whose work belongs more to the "yellow 1890's" than to pre-World War I or to the 1920's, the periods in which his work was largely written.

At first glance, Firbank's small novels seem precious and contrived, and his characters seem exaggerations of the bored and listless Dorian Grays of the *fin de siècle* period. Thus, readers who merely dipped into Firbank and found him not to their liking tended to dismiss him as trivial or anachronistic; but admiring readers tended to join a Firbank cult. That the cult was not always attractive and was often rather silly is exemplified by the *New York Times* review which gushed over Firbank's first American publication (1924) and made glowing reference to the novels still unpublished in America. But the writer of the review did not take his subject seriously enough to check on the other titles very carefully, and the result was that he advised his readers to find Firbank's *Vermouth,* an absurd (and, one must admit, comic) slipup for *Valmouth.* Firbank was "in" in a small circle which admired his camp and could appreciate the allusions with which the pages are studded.

But the old lady from Dubuque (or Sutton Hoo, for that matter) was not likely to be inspired to read Firbank on the basis of such recommendations, while the trend toward increasing naturalism in fiction during the first three decades of the twentieth century set the pattern for novels to which the serious reader was attracted. Firbank remained obscure—so obscure that during his lifetime he could rarely find a publisher willing to pay for the production of one of his novels, and so paid for almost all of them himself. Recently, Firbank's work has become available in attractive editions,[2] and it is possible to find out easily whether he is a charming anachronism or, as Wilson asserted, a "classic."

The pages of Firbank's novels are so packed with wit and delightful absurdity that it seems, at first glance, an easy thing to establish his peculiar style by quoting liberally and letting the quotations speak for themselves. This is not entirely true, for quotations out of context are likely to heighten a critic's impression that Firbank is merely precious and that he is trying too hard. Occasionally, it is undeniable that Firbank overloads a novel with *bon mots* and "comic" dialogue that are not always comical; but he succeeds most of the time in all of his novels, and comes very close to succeeding all of the time in some of the late work.

Firbank has usually been classified as a satirist by readers who did take him seriously, but to be a satirist the writer must exhibit a reasonably strong disapproval of those elements of society which he chooses to satirize, and Firbank does not. He led a life which was very much like that lived by some of his characters, and he led that life by choice and deliberate contrivance. Most of his characters live behind elaborate façades, which may lead one to believe that Firbank is satirizing the man beneath the façade; but the façade is so obvious, so exaggerated and contrived, that it becomes the character; and the man beneath the façade disappears into insignificance. Firbank certainly saw that life was very like the sideshows in Vanity Fair; if one wishes to take his men and women, all regular visitors to and participants in Vanity Fair, as satirical representations of society, he may do so; but such broad generalizations about the author's motives are unwise.

Firbank is much given to absurd aphorism. His aphorisms are short, concise sentences expressing a "truth or precept" as the dictionary says they should; but the "truths" which they express exist only in Firbank's imaginary world. These "aphorisms" are eminently quotable, in much the same way that the aphoristic writing of Oscar Wilde or Benjamin Disraeli is quotable. But Wilde and Disraeli wrote about a world which was reasonably normal—if occasionally overglamorized or fashionably decadent. Men and women in their works say witty things because wit is a kind of status symbol; the witty man gained in the eyes of his acquaintances *because* of his wit. In Firbank's world the wit is usually the result of juxtaposed comments or of simple bitchery.

One character may say something rather inconsequential which seems very witty because it is juxtaposed against another, thoroughly absurd remark. All of Firbank's women, for example, say "quotable" things; but they are usually catty: one woman remarks of a friend, "Either she is growing old, or her maid is getting clumsy . . . ," while her friend has just said of the same woman, "You'd never credit it, dear, but we were the same age once." At every turn a reputation dies. Firbank's dialogue is largely gossipy in tone; the reader is sitting in on a conversation in which most of what is being said is not intended for the ears of the world. Wilde and Disraeli have their characters proudly displaying their *bon mots;* Firbank has his characters whispering them to one another.

And, as I have said, the world of Wilde and Disraeli is reasonably normal; but, in the one of Firbank's novels, the natural laws of society are all askew. A Firbank heroine is generally beautiful, extremely sensitive, very rich, or is in such a position in life that she does not need to think about money at all. A Firbank hero is generally beautiful and extremely sensitive; and, if he isn't rich, someone comes along to take care of him. Firbank's men and women do not come up against the *sturm und drang* of the world, unless exaggerated fretting about one's complexion or the hang of a garment can be classified as *sturm und drang.* These epicene, yet always attractive, men and women are not out of place in the Firbank world for it is one in which you can suggest as party favors "vanity bags for the gentlemen and mustache-brushes for the ladies."

And many of the ladies have a slight touch of mustache, and many of the men make use of the contents of vanity bags. It is as though Firbank had done away with the whole problem of gender and substituted for it mere sexuality—albeit sexuality handled with kid gloves. When women are attracted to men, the attraction is likely to be unusual—such as that of a century-old woman of position for a husky farm laborer in his teens. Laura de Nazianzi,

the "saintly" heroine of *The Flower Beneath the Foot*, is in love
with the Prince of Pisuerga; but it is only a dalliance on the
Prince's part, and the result of the affair is that Laura seeks solace
in a most unusual nunnery where Lesbianism is rampant. There is
not a single happy marriage in all of Firbank's work, unless one
may count as happy those marriages in which all pretense of normal relations has disappeared.

Firbank's technique is often that of the "stream-of-consciousness" writers of the first thirty years of this century. Just as they
employed interior monologues or snatches of a conversation to
give an impression of a whole scene, Firbank frequently employs
bits of conversation to give the reader the impression that he is
standing on a balcony overlooking a scene. Occasionally, his characters are given genuine stream-of-consciousness interior monologues which remind one both of James Joyce and Virginia Woolf.
In Firbank's work the reader is always a *voyeur*, watching and
overhearing things which he probably shouldn't see or hear. Often
the overheard conversations do not make literal sense, but Firbank is a master at making a few words suggest whole paragraphs
of meaning. Occasionally, he suggests a great deal by omitting
words altogether, as in this example where two women are alone
in a boat:

'Oh, Olga!'
'Oh, Vi!'
'. . . I hope you've enough money for the boat, dear? . . . ?'
'. . . !!?'
'Tell me, Olga: Is my hat all sideways?'
'. . . . .'

The passage is quoted exactly as it appears in *The Flower Beneath the Foot*. In another novel, Firbank manages to capture the
misery of Miss O'Brookomore upon the receipt of a letter from her
"friend" Mabel which contains the news that Mabel has eloped;
the following is the complete Chapter XX of *Inclinations*:

'Mabel! Mabel! Mabel! Mabel!
Mabel! Mabel! Mabel! Mabel!'

One can see in this sort of thing the refinement of the stream-of-
consciousness technique into a splendid absurdity.

Anthony Powell, in his preface to *The Complete Ronald Firbank*, notes that there are scenes in the novels which are "a foreshadowing of *Finnegans Wake* . . . in the association of ideas." This statement is certainly true, and one might add that the long interior monologue of an old crone in *Concerning the Eccentricities of Cardinal Pirelli* is even more like a burlesque of Molly Bloom's monologue at the end of *Ulysses*. There are similarities, too, in the way in which both Firbank and Joyce look upon the world as a great comic stage; but, where Joyce is raucously vulgar, Firbank is effeminately refined or relies upon *double entendres*. Where Joyce penetrates deep into the heart of a very real Dublin, Firbank penetrates into the heartless, superrefined world of imaginary courts and *salons*. Though the two writers deal with entirely different levels of society, the resulting scenes are often similar in their allusiveness and in their sense of movement and life. And both writers create scenes in which humans become grotesques.

It would be silly to insist that Firbank's work ever really approaches Joyce's in its complexity and density, yet there is often in it a denseness of imagery and incident which makes his novels read slowly. One cannot race through them, just as one cannot race through *Ulysses;* and the richness of any of Firbank's mature works makes it necessary to take them in smallish doses. One is fearful of "missing something," of overlooking a fine pun or *bon mot;* but, of course, to read Firbank with such seriousness is to destroy the marvelous effect which he labored so hard to create. William Butler Yeats, in "Adam's Curse," says of poetry, "A line will take us hours maybe;/Yet if it does not seem a moment's thought,/Our stitching and unstitching has been naught." Firbank must have felt much the same way, for he labored to achieve the casual effect of flashing brilliance that marks his work, and which seems to be the "moment's thought" of a witty mind.[3]

Aside from its similarities to the stream-of-consciousness techniques, other significant characteristics of Firbank's style may be noted. He is likely to sprinkle his paragraphs with French and German phrases, and, occasionally, a phrase from a less familiar language. Generally, these phrases are taken from current chic jargon, which gives the effect of listening in on the conversations of extremely worldly people, and heightens our sense of the international nature of the characters. Just as the wealthy and well-educated people of most countries resemble one another more than the poor and uneducated of one country resemble the poor and uneducated of another, so Firbank's characters generally resemble worldly and well-educated Englishmen, or Americans, or Frenchmen. They are international and sophisticated, rather than local and parochial. Furthermore, Firbank uses foreign words and phrases to make innuendoes and occasional puns. But the real reason is to add *ton* to the dialogue, just as the word *ton* added *ton* to many a Victorian dialogue.

Firbank's descriptive similes and allusions are more in number than those which may be found in a similar number of pages from any novelist writing in English except Joyce. They are always exaggerated and unlikely. The effect, often, is to make one stop abruptly to savor the absurdity of the simile at the expense of whatever plot there might be. One may open Firbank's works at random and come upon them. This one, for example, from *Vainglory* describes Saint Dorothy's Cathedral, the setting of several incidents in the novel: "Miss Massingham, in her *Sacredotalism and Satanism*, has called the whole thing heavy, '*Very weighty indeed*,' although she willingly admits that at twilight the towers, with their many pinnacles, become utterly fantastic, *like the helmets of eunuchs in carnival time*. But then, if there was not much spontaneity about them on the whole, they had taken a long time to build. Stone towers cannot be dashed off like Fragonard's *Inspiration*."

The comparison of the towers at twilight to the carnival helmets of eunuchs is a typical example of Firbank's use of the absurd simile. His citing of the fictitious Miss Massingham as the ultimate authority on ecclesiastical architecture is also a typical device; and the "lady's" description is, taken altogether, a fine burlesque of the Baedecker style that was popular at the end of the nineteenth century. Finally, there is the reference to the real Fragonard which is the ultimate absurdity, for it would be impossible to imagine any artist whose style would be less likely to come to mind to provide a comparison with a Gothic Cathedral. The resulting paragraph is a combination of unlikely allusions juxtaposed against one another, and all in a most serious tone. This is the sort of thing at which Firbank excels, and which has been properly labelled as camp.

Firbank's allusions are as likely to be to imaginary artists or authorities as to actual ones. Occasionally he alludes to a real artist, such as Raphael, but attributes to him an imaginary picture such as "The Madonna with a hoe" which is described as an "exquisite variation of 'La Belle Jardiniere.'" There are as many allusions to music as there are to paintings and artists. Obviously, Firbank knew music very well, and especially opera, which, with its melodrama and opportunities for inherent absurdity, particularly attracted him. For example, in one novel, *Inclinations*, one may find references to (among many others) both *Tannhäuser* and *Cunegunde*, one a real and one an imaginary opera. Many of the novels tell of performances of specific arias ranging from one which begins "Gaze not on swans" from *Leda*, to the actual "Depuis la jour" from Charpentier's *Louise*.

On several occasions we meet the composers of new operas, such as Winsome Brookes who is writing *Justinian* which opens on a scene full of people "grouped invalidishly about the great doorway of Santa Sophia." On another occasion we hear of someone who has sung, in church, Tosca's "Vissi d'arte," in which the heroine tells her would-be seducer that she lives only for art and love. The young and distinctly decadent hero of *Lady Appledore's Mésalliance* spends an evening at Covent Garden swooning through *Tristan und Isolde*, while someone else says, grotesquely, "I just love the Isolde cocktail music from *Tristan*, when it's jazzed, don't you?" The reply she receives is just as silly: "I never know one Opera, darling, from another. Isn't that the one with Fricka's rams?" Wagner's massive *Tristan* and his *Ring* operas are reduced to the confused chitchat of a gossip session. Richard Strauss's spectacular and "decadent" *Salome* furnishes the theme for an entire novel in which the heroine, obviously under the influence of the opera, seeks a John the Baptist of her own.

Firbank's references to these works, when they are not deliberately ironic or perverse, are always knowledgeable and show him to be acquainted with a large number of composers, though most of them may be broadly characterized as Romantic. All of the composers wrote works which are grand and melodramatic (such as Wagner) or which belong either in style or in subject matter, in the broadest sense, to the decadence of the late nineteenth century (such as Debussy's *Pelleas* and Richard Strauss's *Salome*). Composers whose chief works are symphonic are rarely men-

tioned, and this is understandable, for Firbank's own work is of
the theatrical sort which makes it more akin to opera than to sym-
phonies.

The settings of the novels range from England to the West Indies. While these places are identifiable, they are certainly not
accurately drawn, nor are they intended to be real. Firbank himself, in his preface to *The Flower Beneath the Foot*, explains the
reasons for this more clearly than anyone else could do:

I suppose the Flower beneath the Foot is really Oriental in origin,
although the scene is some imaginary Vienna. The idea came in
Algeria while writing Santal. . . . A kind of nostalgia (which *may*
only have been waywardness) turned all my thoughts toward Vienna,
And it was a veritable craving for Vienna, too. I remember it was at
Touggourt in mid-Sahara while assisting at a sunset from the minaret
of a Mosque, that I found the Duchess of Varna's courtdress—the
green of Nile water. . . . Ah, the East . . . I propose to return
there, some day, when I write about New York.[4]

One may clearly see from this statement that Firbank found
places more intriguing when viewed from the distance and from a
situation which was alien or foreign to the subject about which he
was writing. Because of this penchant, his settings are more like
stage-sets—or like places seen in a dream. The Vienna of *The
Flower Beneath the Foot* would scarcely be recognized by a Vien-
nese, just as the romantic beauty of New York in *The New
Rythum* is scarcely recognizable to a New Yorker. In reality, all of
Firbank's settings are "Oriental" in the sense that they are not
truly European. There is a Surrealistic quality about them in that
we see momentary references to real things that are familiar. In
The New Rythum we read of the Bronx (used incidentally, without the "The" which is always a part of its name), but we find it in
a New York City which is described in this way: "It was a pink
and elusive evening towards the break of Easter, Zephyr and
Flora caressed New York, yearned above her glimmering parks
and gardens, brooded above her budding avenues (awakening
young chestnut-leaf and brooding lilac), rippled that way, this
way, all caprice. . . ."[5] It is far finer to think of Third Avenue
lined with budding "brooding lilacs" than covered with the ugly
elevated tracks which then decorated it. This New York—full of
gardens and flowers, and caressed by Zephyr and Flora—is

obviously the creation of one who had never seen the city except in his imagination.

Sometimes, Firbank describes scenery as though it were an elaborate costume clothing the earth. It is frequently implied that the scenery is in good or bad taste ("A smart, plain sky stretched starless above St. Dorothy. . . ."), just as the clothes his characters wear are described in relation to their good or bad taste. Everything in the world of these novels is artificial, and the reader in search of genuine satire should be warned that, though satire is there, it is of a very special sort and seems to show that Firbank often admired, even while he laughed, many of the objects of his satire.

Firbank's bawdiness is another matter. It is often possible to read *double entendres* into a phrase. These bawdy phrases are almost all handled with considerable wit and delicacy, but there is no question about the fact that a reader who misses the *double entendres* misses a good deal of Firbank. We may look at many of the scenes and incidents as manifestations of Firbank's own sexual interests, but to submit his work to such "Freudian" analysis would be to destroy the fragile wit in them. Suffice it to say that homosexuality, flagellation, and nymphomania play large roles in these novels, as we shall see when we deal with them individually.

Firbank's view of the world is that of one who sees the irony of human existence. On the one hand, there are death and decay (both of which he treats with ironic humor); on the other, there is the importance of always appearing at one's best. Life is always a little game in the mature novels, where one-upsmanship is as important as questions of faith or survival. His contemporaries, almost to a man, also saw these ironic contrasts; but they chose to treat them as evidence of human depravity, whereas Firbank chose to see the *comedy* inherent in them.

II *Up from the Mines*

Only three family generations before Ronald Firbank visited the bookstores in London's Charing Cross Road with his fingernails tinted a delicate pink, his great-grandfather had worked in the mines of County Durham in the dour North of England. Only two generations before Ronald Firbank haunted the "esthetic" Café Royal, observing the elegant Bohemian life of that place, his grandfather had worked as a common laborer on a new railway line. And only one generation after his *nouveau riche* father had declared himself "keen on sports" in *Who's Who*, Ronald Firbank decked himself out in ridiculous sports attire and practiced running for the sake of his figure.

It would be almost impossible to imagine, at first glance, a family background less likely to produce a delicate, witty writer like Ronald Firbank, whose pen dwelt lovingly over the details of feminine dress and feminine gossip, than the combination of illiteracy, physical vigor, and philistinism which did, in fact, produce him. I say "at first glance" because we may, if we look beneath the surface of things, find that the fantastically fast rise of the Firbank family fortunes, from illiterate miner to magnate to MP in three generations, logically culminated in the young man whose effeminate manners and esthetic inclinations marked the "decadence" of this vigorous advancement. It is a short family history, but of the greatest possible interest to both the student of literature and the psychologist.

Thomas Firbank, Ronald's great-grandfather, was an illiterate coal miner in County Durham in the town of Bishop Auckland. It is intriguing, if academic, to wonder what his impressions of his great-grandson would have been; perhaps he was a mute Milton whose spirit, transformed from Milton to Oscar Wilde, reincarnated itself in Ronald, but one can only conjecture romantically about such things. His great-grandson had absolutely no inclinations toward the simple life (if the grinding misery of a nineteenth-century miner's life may be called "simple"), and in his novels there is no hint of any curiosity about County Durham. Neighboring Yorkshire appears in one novel as a comically desolate place from which one of his heroines awaits delivery, but that is the only significant reference to the North from which his family came.

The extraordinary rise of the Firbank fortunes began with Joseph Firbank who was the apotheosis of the self-made man. He went to work in the mines at Bishop Auckland at the age of seven, and the pattern was set for another generation—or, following the natural order of things, *should* have been set. Joseph Firbank was, however, a man of such vigor and imagination that he aspired, in the truest sense of that word, to a new life for himself and his heirs. He left the mines to become a common laborer on the new railway line which was being built from Bishop Auckland to

Weardale. This got him out of the pits but, obviously, scarcely improved his finances or social standing, yet it was the first symbolic step from obscurity to the bright light in which he and the next generations came to live.

We must look upon that era, the 1850's, as a time of limitless horizons for a man of energy and uninhibited drive for advancement. The railroads which were spreading over England provided the opportunity for a young man who was willing to seize it; Joseph Firbank did, taking a subcontract for one of the tunnels on the new line. He was successful enough to leave County Durham in 1854 to work for the Monmouthshire Railway and Canal Company at Newport in the West of England. Though he never lost his North country accent and brusque ways, this date marks the end of the Firbank family's real connections with the North. In his memoir of Ronald Firbank, I. K. Fletcher relates several anecdotes, one of which shows how tenaciously Joseph Firbank's Durham accent remained with him, and illustrates, as well, his pragmatic view of life. His son, Ronald's father, enjoyed hunting, a pleasure which Joseph, with his respect for hard work, did not share. One day he visited the company stables and found that his son had put "a spruce hunter in the stables with the cart-horses." One can imagine the frown, the moment of pregnant silence, and, finally, the dry remark: "Eh, lad! That woarnt pull a load o' muck!" [6]

Though his grandson was removed from "loads o' muck," as far as one could possibly be removed from such things, the two men in their photos bear a striking resemblance to one another. The younger man's features are delicate versions of his grandparent's coarser, but handsome features. The imagination and vigor which Joseph Firbank used to become one of the richest contractors in England was thoroughly transformed and passed on to Ronald Firbank whose imagination created a whole world, and whose delicate vigor was expended entirely upon his art.

Thirty-two years after Joseph had left County Durham, he died in Newport and left a fortune which Mr. Fletcher describes as "immense." The contracting business was inherited by his oldest son, Joseph Thomas Firbank, who later dropped the Joseph and was known as Thomas Firbank. This man, Ronald's father, was to raise the social position of the family considerably. The 1905 edition of *Who's Who* shows this entry: "FIRBANK, Sir Joseph

Thomas, Kt., cr. 1902 [Knight, created 1902]; M. P. (C.) Hull, E. [Member of Parliament, Conservative, for Hull East]. . . . a Director of Union Assurance Society, Newport (Monmouthshire) Gas Works, and of Wembley Tower Company; Chairman Old Delabole Slate Company, Cornwall; *Recreations*, very keen on all outdoor sports and athletics, music and objects of art. . . . *Clubs:* Carlton, Union, Junior Carlton, White's, Junior Constitutional." Some of the juxtapositions in this paragraph (director of a gas works and collector of *objets d'art*) might have been created by Sir Thomas's son for one of his novels. The real interest by the *Who's Who* entry is that it shows how the Firbank family, though very much on the rise, still retained some ties with its simpler past.

Sir Thomas married Jane Garret, the daughter of an Irish clergyman, who was "sensitive and attached to lovely things." [7] This woman, Ronald Firbank's mother, was the most important influence upon her son's career. Ronald always admired his mother enormously, and was, in fact, perhaps unnaturally dependent upon her. Photographs of Lady Firbank show a beautiful woman who gives the impression of stateliness and, at the same time, of good nature. She was always sure of her son's cleverness and apparently was always proud of his books. Had she not introduced him to art and to beautiful things when he was a child, it is conceivable that Firbank's life might have taken another direction. She protected him and surrounded him with lavish affection, even at the expense of incurring the ridicule of some of Ronald's contemporaries. When he was nineteen, for example, she took the special precaution of preparing a room for him at his tutor's by sending around "a footman and a housemaid . . . with a new bed, complete with eiderdown and a special armchair." [8]

Part of Lady Firbank's solicitous attitude toward her son was due to the fact that he had never been strong, having contracted a weakness of the lungs as a small child. His physical weakness contributed to the hit-or-miss quality of his education, for he found life in a boy's school very nearly impossible and stayed at the first one he attended, Uppingham, less than a year. From Uppingham, Firbank went to Tours to learn French; and Fletcher tells us of his period that "He learned French, and, more important, he studied French literature. He read Maeterlinck, Baudelaire, Mallarmé, Flaubert, Gautier, and Henri de Regnier. His education was not only literary but liberal. He acquired the graceful habit of wearing ties from Doucet's and from Carvet's. He felt for the first time the attraction of the Roman Catholic religion. And he found in the scenery of Touraine the focus of his growing literary powers." [9] In 1905, he published in a single volume at his own expense *Odette d'Antrevernes* and *A Study in Temperament.*

Firbank went next to Spain to learn Spanish, then to a tutor to prepare for Cambridge, and, finally, in 1906 to Cambridge itself. He was, obviously, ill-prepared intellectually and emotionally to contend with life at the university. He chose Trinity Hall as his college, "in those days . . . chiefly a college of rowing, hunting, and racing men who seldom passed examinations successfully." [10] In this vigorously masculine world, Firbank devoted most of his time to the decoration of his room, to visits to the University Museum, and to trips to London to see whatever was then most *au courant.* He did attempt, however, to do something in the athletic line at Trinity Hall; for the London *Daily Mirror* of February 5, 1908,[11] had a photograph of a Trinity Hall race in which Firbank, incredibly enough, is one of the starters. It is entirely possible that he thought of the race as a good way of keeping slim rather than as a worthwhile bit of competition.

III   *Firbank's Conversion*

During Firbank's stay at Cambridge, in 1908 to be precise, he apparently entered the Roman Catholic Church, at least according to Professor E. J. Dent. To my mind there is some doubt about this, for Firbank is reported to have said to Lord Berners that "The Church of Rome wouldn't have me and so I mock at her." [12] What did Firbank mean by this curious remark if, indeed, he had been received into the Church? Perhaps he was referring to the fact that he had been unable, later, to find a post at the Vatican as he had wanted to do; but doubts about Firbank's actual affiliation with the church are heightened by his own extremely mocking tone when dealing with it in all of the post-Cambridge novels. Apparently almost no one else knew that Firbank was a Roman Catholic: for, when he died in Rome in 1926, he was buried in the Protestant Cemetery, though the body was later disinterred and removed to the Catholic cemetery. Whatever Firbank's connection with Roman Catholicism was, it was unorthodox; for his novels are filled with impious priests and corrupt saints and Lesbianic nuns. It *is* very likely that the elaborate hierarchy of the

Roman Church and its magnificent ritual appealed to him, but it is improbable that he was a practicing Catholic. In fact, it is known that he fell, for a time, under the influence (at least superficially) of "wizards" and practitioners of "black magic." Since he was little inclined to make his position clear to his friends about such matters, considerable doubt still exists about his religious life and his actual connection with the Church of Rome.

Firbank left Cambridge in 1909 without having taken a single examination during his stay there. This casual approach to academic life should not imply, however, that he did nothing of intellectual value while at the university; for he read avidly, finding special pleasure in the works of the French Decadents. Fletcher remarks that "this was his Impressionist period," and an acquaintance from that time has recorded exactly how impressionable Firbank was: " 'His sensitiveness was such that it was obvious when one saw him what book he had last been reading—especially, of course, if it was something very strong like *Hamlet* or *Volpone,* when he would behave like Hamlet or Volpone, and speak to one almost as if he were Hamlet or Volpone.' " [13] In addition to Shakespeare and Jonson, "Dowson and Condor, Arthur Symons and Beardsley were his chief joys," [14] outside of the French writers.

After Cambridge, Firbank led a nomadic life visiting Egypt, Paris, and Vienna. Egypt was suitably exotic, and he made several visits there, choosing Cairo as the place in which to begin his last novel, *The New Rythum* (which was not completed), set in New York City. The death of Sir Thomas Firbank in 1910 plunged the family into financial difficulties, for the family fortune was considerably less than anyone had imagined it to be. For a time, it looked as if Ronald would have to find some orthodox kind of job; but, in fact, this extremity never came to pass, and he continued to live as though money meant absolutely nothing to him. Though the family was no longer boundlessly wealthy, it was not in anything approaching straitened circumstances by any ordinary standards.

In Paris, Firbank met many of the glamorous Montmartre figures of pre-World War I days; and in London he frequented the bars and cafés of smart Bohemia, and especially the Café Royal (which is the splendidly ludicrous setting of a scene in *Caprice*) and Le Tour Eiffel located "on the outskirts of Tottenham Court Road as though to give a masochistic stimulation of ugliness to its aesthetic clientele." [15] At the cafés he was most frequently in the company of men such as Augustus John and Evan Morgan, but he enjoyed, too, the proximity of the less distinguished clientele:

At the Café Royal, when on a race night he sat, pink cheek by heavy jowl, with the exulting bookmakers and heard their coarse witticisms as he twisted his glass with carmined fingers, his pleasure was intense. In his own time he finished his drink, set down his glass with a gesture which emphasized his limp elegance, casually drew out a wad of banknotes and paid his bill. With malicious enjoyment he noticed how the small eyes of his neighbors narrowed with avarice and how ingratiating smiles crept upon their faces. When one of them passed the time of day with him his triumph was complete.[16]

His eccentricities during this period of his life were becoming increasingly prominent. He had begun to drink heavily and to eat very little. Part of his eating habits (he once ate a single green pea at a banquet) were the result of his self-dramatizing personality, but they were equally the result of his fantastic nervousness and shyness which caused him to break out in fits of laughter when he attempted to tell a story or take part in a conversation.

In 1912 Osbert Sitwell recalled having seen him at theatrical performances in London, a "lonely, stooping, rather absurd figure of a man" who seemed to be "a witty and decadent Red Indian." [17] Firbank's wit was generally lying dormant during this time, it seems, for he was doing no writing. Instead, he was making the rounds of the fashionable world, observing and storing up the images which he would transform in a few years into scenes in his novels. Certainly, he was "difficult," especially when he had been drinking heavily; and he could become offensive, refusing to meet someone because he was "ugly" or flying into rages against his friends over imagined slights. Sometimes he tried his friends' patience with absurd whims, such as his insistence that Evan Morgan was really a reincarnation of Rameses, which led him to drag Morgan off to the British Museum to see "his original" whenever they met.[18]

It would be easy to dwell on these eccentricities at great length, for they give us a picture not only of Firbank but of some of the peculiarities which could flower in a period not far removed from that of the Decadents. But beneath this eccentric behavior lurked, by the common agreement of all who knew him, a gentle and kind man who would have enjoyed conventional friendships had he been able to handle them psychologically. The eccentricities contributed in an odd way to Firbank's literary career; for since they to a large extent isolated him from society, he lived in an imaginary world which became the one in which his characters finally came to life.

IV   Publication of the First Novels

Vainglory appeared in 1915 and was followed by *Inclinations* in 1916; a revision of the early *Odette* the same year; *Caprice*, 1917; *Valmouth*, 1919; *The Princess Zoubaroff* (a play), 1920; and *Santal*, 1921. Though there is some variation in the quality of these works (*Santal* is, by far, the poorest), they are somewhat of a piece for they were written either in whole or in part while Firbank was escaping from the visible evidences of World War I. London was too full of khaki and war news, so he finally retired to Oxford where he felt that he could live in isolation from the "unpleasantness" and yet get to London in an hour or so, should an interesting theatrical performance manage to appear amid wartime restrictions. Needless to say, the draft board had found him totally unfit for service, though the inefficiencies of bureaucracy caused the board to call him up for examination time after time. Osbert Sitwell tells of one humorous result of this error.

The constant callings-up and medical examinations had . . . further shattered his health, just as he, in return, must have somewhat shattered the health of the various military authorities with whom he came into contact. He told us, for example, that when, after a dozen or so examinations, the War Office finally rejected him as totally unfit for service (which anyone else could have told at a glance), and then, in their usual muddled way, at once called him up again, he replied to them through his lawyer with the threat of a libel action. The War Office, at a time when it governed the world, was so taken aback at this simple piece of individual initiative that it at once sent back to him a humble apology.[19]

Firbank immersed himself in pleasant surroundings at Oxford and entered into that period in his life which was to be his most productive. He dropped the "Arthur" from his name and became simply "Ronald Firbank," and he also went to work on *Vainglory* and the other novels of the wartime period. After the war, he attempted to return to his old life; but of course, though he had not changed, the world had; and he was never again at ease. He continued to travel widely (including a trip to Haiti), and he spent as much time as he could at the theaters. When Aldous Huxley met him at about this time, he recorded his impressions:

'I used to see him from time to time at the theatre when I was doing dramatic criticism. He often attended First Nights, in spite of an overwhelming shyness which made the presence of other people an agony to him. Sometimes the agony was so great that he would do extraordinary things that made him very conspicuous and so increased his self-consciousness, (e.g. he would get up in the middle of an act, or start rummaging under his seat). He must have derived some curious painful pleasure from his embarrassments. The last time I saw him was at Robert Nichols' wedding. We sat with various other people in the Café Royal. As I took my seat at the table opposite him, Firbank gave his usual agonized wriggle of embarrassment and said:
        ' "Aldous—always my *torture*." ' [20]

Firbank completed three more novels, *The Flower Beneath the Foot* (1923); *Prancing Nigger* which was published in 1924 in America and was the first of his books which made money; and *Concerning the Eccentricities of Cardinal Pirelli*, for which he went to Spain for inspiration, and which was published just after his death in 1926.

Firbank's death was a lonely and sad one. His mother, whom he loved so much, had died in 1924; and he had a growing sense of his own approaching old age. He went to Egypt to begin work on his "American" novel and then, finally, to Rome. In Rome it had been his habit, on all of his visits, to "rent some huge and generally rather gloomy apartment, where he would live in absolute solitude." [21] Even the servants were required to be invisible. Lord Berners tells of an acquaintance who lived across the courtyard from one of Firbank's Rome apartments and "sometimes in the depths of the night he would hear through the open windows the sound of chuckling and laughter coming from the lonely inmate of the apartment vis-à-vis." [22] Firbank died with no one in attendance but his doctor. In *Vainglory*, he wrote of Winsome Brookes who, due to his manner of dressing, "suggested sometimes. . . .a St. Sebastian with too many arrows." The image, both comic and horrible, makes one think of Firbank himself and of his life, full of the grotesque and the pathetic.

CHAPTER 2

Practicing

I *Earliest Works*

ODETTE D'ANTREVERNES, The Artificial Princess and *Inclinations,* three short novels, show Firbank experimenting, both with technique and with subject matter. There can be no doubt that he only intermittently found his proper *milieu* in these three works. One of them, *The Artificial Princess,* seems to be a mature product; but, since it may have been revised near the end of his life, it is likely that the stylistic maturity that we find in it is, at least partially, the product of that period rather than of his early period. In any event, the three short novels provide an interesting introduction to his work; for they contain in them at least the seeds of all of the better, later novels.

Strictly speaking, none of these books are true novels for they are far too short. The longest of them, *Inclinations,* is a little under one hundred pages; and the shortest, *Odette,* is only ten pages long. Thus we are faced with the problem of classifying them. Technically, we may call *Odette* a short story; *The Artificial Princess,* a long short story or a novella; and *Inclinations,* a short novel. To avoid the problem of stumbling over such classifications, all three will, however, be referred to as novels. The reason for this extremely simplified classification is convenience, nothing more.

Throughout all of his work, we find constant reminders of Firbank's familiarity with the literature of the Decadence and *fin de siècle* period. In these three novels we are frequently reminded of this era in the references to costume design that show an affinity with the taste of Aubrey Beardsley, the conscientious "naughtiness" that is everywhere evident, and the frequent *ennui* that afflicts some of the characters. What sets Firbank apart from most of the Decadent writers is the wit with which he approaches these matters. What is serious in Hûysmans is usually ludicrous in Firbank, and the sins of characters like Wilde's Dorian Gray are turned into harmless absurdities in Firbank's work, even in these early works—except in *Odette d'Antrevernes* where Firbank seems to want us to take his story seriously.

It is clear that Firbank is a literary rebel; he is adept at lifting the mannerisms of writers of several different schools and transforming them into absurdities. Though he admired the writers who were conscientiously *fin de siècle*, we sense that his admiration is that of a young person for some very glamorous older person. By the time he reached full literary maturity, he was capable of mocking everyone from Byron to Baudelaire. And a note should be made here of a Firbank technique that is reminiscent of Pope: the use of juxtaposition. Pope, in *The Rape of the Lock*, for example, couples the significant with the trivial in a single line, thus "wretches hang that jury-men may dine" and women weep with equal violence for the death of a lap-dog or a husband. Firbank employs this technique of juxtaposition frequently for humorous effect. Two of the three early novels under consideration show many of these characteristics, though not so thoroughly as later works.

Odette d'Antrevernes, unfortunately, does not give any indication of Firbank's later work, with the exception of a short novel written in Tunis a decade and a half later, *Santal. Odette* should, apparently, be taken seriously. It is no more than a short story, and it indicates Firbank's early interest in the Roman Catholic Church, for which he seems to have had a strong affinity, especially for its mystical elements. His stories abound in miracles and references to saints (though the miracles are usually ludicrous and the saints of, at best, dubious piety). In any event, there is no real evidence to indicate that Firbank was indulging in a piece of fantastic camp when he wrote *Odette,* though the absurdity (apparently unconscious) of the heroine and her story is monumental.

Odette is a highly moralistic little story with some decadent overtones. It tells of a pious and romantically inclined orphan who lives in a chateau in the valley of the Loire. She says things "in her pretty baby voice" like "I have been listening to the birds saying their evening prayers." She is under the influence of an old Curé whose name is Bois-Fleuri, and she has spent her childhood in the Convent of the Holy Dove where she enjoyed hearing of St. Bernadette: "Oh! how Odette wished that she could have been little Bernadette! And she would delight to surmise what the little

peasant girl looked like; whether her hair was brown, or whether
it was gold—and Odette was terribly disappointed when asking
the Curé this question, that he only shook his head and said he
did not know." [1]

But her interest in St. Bernadette extends beyond a mere curiosity about her appearance: "Then one beautiful evening in August,
as little Odette watched the two twin towers of the distant Cathedral flush purple in the setting sun, and the great dome of St. Martin's Church loom like a ripe apricot against the sky, a wonderful
idea came to her. She, too, would seek the Holy Virgin. She, too,
like little Bernadette, would speak with the Holy Mary, the
Mother of the Lord Seigneur Christ." [2]

Odette prays for a week in preparation for her vision of the
Virgin Mary, and finally she goes one night into the garden in
order to be ready. Hearing a moan, she assumes that she is about
to see the Mother of Christ; but it turns out to be a "woman with
painted cheeks and flaming hair." Ten years later, Firbank would
have made this incident a richly comic perversion of a pious
scene with all kinds of mistaken identities, but little Odette is earnest. She gives the woman a silver cross and asks of her, "Will you
promise never to do things that the Holy Mother would not approve of?" The hussy is repentant and tears fall from her eyes; and
all of nature rejoices with Odette and her convert: "Far away in
the East, the day began to Dawn. A flush of yellow like ripe fruit
spread slowly across the sky. The birds in the trees piped drowsily
to one another, and the bent cyclamens by the riverside lifted
their fragrant hearts in rapture to the rising sun." [3]

The painted woman goes her way, promising to "find work—
honest work . . . And then, with a tired, sad step, the woman
walked slowly away down the long white road, her shadow falling
beside her as though it were her soul." And Odette, watching her,
derives a lesson: ". . . suddenly she realised that Life was not a
dream; she realised that Life was cruel, that Life was sad, that
beyond the beautiful garden in which she dwelt, many millions of
people were struggling to live, and sometimes in the struggle for
life one failed. . . ." [4]

This sententious stuff would seem to be written with tongue in
cheek; the heavy Victorian tone is completely out of harmony
with Firbank's usual frame of mind, both in the contemporary
Study in Temperament and in all the later novels. Fallen women

in a Firbank novel are not converted into industrious Victorian
ladies by the pleas of charming little girls. We would like to think
that Firbank is satirizing every moralistic tale that came out of the
nineteenth century and, along with the stories, their heroines—all
the precocious Little Nells and Sweet Annies who provided inspiration for thousands of readers. But it isn't a satire—it is merely a
case of his having made a serious mistake. We must not judge
Odette in the light of the later novels; for, if we do, we are bound
to come to the conclusion that it *must* be a satire.

The story concludes with a suitably dramatic sunrise, symbolic
of both hope and redemption: "And Odette turned as she walked,
and looked behind her, to where, by the roadside, and dying beneath the golden sun, the red roses that she had gathered for the
Holy Mother, shone in the morning light like drops of crimson
blood." [5] The rich descriptions of flowers and the "drops of crimson blood" show that Firbank is still being *fin de siècle* in *Odette*.
It is worth noting that he was a poor imitator. Happily, from this
point on, he is a creator.

II   *Dialogues*

Of all of Firbank's novels, *Inclinations* (1916) is the most difficult to read. It is often fairly troublesome to decide who is speaking, and we are sometimes reduced to counting back to the last
identifying "she said." In the work of another, this might not be
such a problem; but Firbank's characters rarely have speech characteristics which identify them. Furthermore, *Inclinations* is almost *entirely* conversation. A count of the lines of type in which
Chapter I is set (in *The Complete Ronald Firbank*) shows that
there are a total of 273 lines; of these, only forty-five are not parts
of a conversation. This number would not be extraordinarily high
except that in those 273 lines of type, 143 introduce new speeches.
It is very much like reading a play in which the dialogue is very
rapid but in which there are no indications of the speakers' identities. If we add to this characteristic the fact that Firbank's characters tend to reply to one another in irrelevancies, we may see just
how difficult it is to follow the speaker.

Before discussing the content of the novel, it should be noted
that Part II, Chapter IV, of *Inclinations* was revised in 1925 (both
versions are included in the New Directions edition). If we ob-
serve the stylistic differences between the 1916 version and the

1925 version of the same scene, we discover some clear indications
of the direction which Firbank's style took after 1916. In the earlier version, Chapter IV contains eighty paragraphs (counting
each indented passage and "speech" as a paragraph), all but
eleven of which begin with quotation marks. In other words, the
chapter is approximately seven-eighths dialogue. In the 1925 version, Chapter IV has been expanded from eighty to 107 paragraphs: not only are there twenty-seven more paragraphs, but
most of them are considerably longer than the eighty paragraphs
of the original version. In the later version, only fifty-eight paragraphs begin with quotation marks; only slightly more than half
of the chapter is actually dialogue; and the rest is composed almost entirely of descriptions of dresses or of weirdly comic charac-
terizations.

All of this line counting and paragraph counting should provide
a guide, albeit a dull one, to the changes in Firbank's style as he
matured artistically. The extended conversations in the novels
tend to be far less interesting and witty than the overheard bits of
conversation in which we are plunged *in medias res.* Firbank's
style improved as he continued to write, and the high dialogue
content of *Inclinations* was an experiment that didn't prove entirely successful. When one of his fantastic *characters* describes a
scene, it is less absurd, less witty, than when Firbank as the omniscient author, often sounding very much like a gossipy newspaper
"Society" columnist, does the describing.

Inclinations opens at a soirée where the principal guest is Geraldine O'Brookomore, "the authoress of *Six Strange Sisters, Those
Gonzagas,* etc." Miss O'Brookomore is about to begin a new biography of Catherine Kettler ("Kitty" is her intimate name for her
subject) about whom we find out very little, except that "she was
like some radiant milkmaid" and that she was "so English." Her
precocity is indicated by the fact that, at the age of two, she remarked, "I would worship . . . to spend a summer in a hut in a
hollow of Old Sarum." The only extant picture of her is in the
Liechtenstein Gallery, and it shows a woman of "a startling pallor." Miss O'Brookomore is not put off her biography by a friend's
remark upon seeing a replica of the picture: "I wonder at anyone
sitting down to pen the life of a woman so baggy about the eyes!"
In search of material for her biography, Miss O'Brookomore is
planning to journey to Greece where Mrs. Kettler has been

(though it *may* have been Ceylon—Miss O'Brookomore is not exactly sure). Because traveling alone is a bore, "the Biographer" invites Mabel Collins to accompany her.

Mabel Collins is the real heroine of the novel, and her inclinations provide the title. She is a sensitive girl who has spent her life in the wilds of Yorkshire where, she feels, her talents have been unfulfilled, and where her inclinations cannot come to fruition. She and her family are tied to their home because it is so extraordinarily ugly that they can find no one to sublease it. Their only journeys are to Scotland—in the winter. They hope to find, in Scotland, someone who is "pining for the South" and who will, consequently, take their Yorkshire house. Mabel readily accepts Miss O'Brookomore's invitation to accompany her to Greece, though we are given a foreshadowing of the dire events to come when Miss O'Brookomore, musing alone, wonders about the motives behind her hasty invitation to the girl: "Was it solely Vampirism that made me ask her, . . . or is it that I'm simply bored?"

The scene switches briefly to London where we see Miss O'Brookomore encountering her teacher "the veteran Biographer," Mrs. Asp. We are shown a peculiarly countrified Brompton, full of "pastoral plots" and shrubberies and scenes which, collectively, make Miss O'Brookomore think that the scene near Harrod's "that morning seemed extraordinarily Greek." There follows a brief and irrelevant scene in a gallery where Firbank uses his overheard-conversation technique, though with less success than in his later work. Two more very brief chapters, one on a train en route to Marseilles and another on board the ship bound for Athens, do little but show Mabel Collins to be a foolish, flighty, and melodramatic girl. Imagining a funeral on board the ship, she plans a costume and suitable prose: "I dare say I could lean from the ship-side in a silver hat crowned with black Scotch roses." She also meets "Count" Pastorelli of Orvieto who is to be her undoing.

All of this speedy action finally concludes at Athens where we are introduced to many new characters. Mr. and Mrs. Arbanel are having a dreary honeymoon there, and Professor and Mrs. Cowsend are visiting the city so that he may do research. Mrs. Cowsend is a mild satire upon the plain-thinking English lady traveller who can easily find "things in Somerset just as lovely as in the Vale of Tempe." Miss Dawkins, an alcoholic Australian in search of her long-lost parents, is visiting the countries of the world al-

phabetically: ". . . India, Italy, Iceland. . . ." are next on her
itinerary. Miss Arne, "the *only* Lady Teazle," is an actress who has
come to Greece to find inspiration for a new production of *Lysis-
trata*, and she chooses the doltish Miss Dawkins to be her Lam-
pito.

Though there are some men around, and the "Count" is always
hovering in the background, the company is to all intents and
purposes feminine. When the women decide to pass their time
with a pleasant duck hunt at Salamis, the venture ends in disaster;
for the addlepated, jealous bride, Mrs. Arbanel, shoots Miss Arne
instead of a duck. Tragedy, then, rounds off the day; and Miss
Collins is given a chance to wear the silver hat with "black Scotch
roses" though there is, unfortunately, no ship from which to lean
gracefully.

The Athens pilgrimmage concludes with another tragedy, at
least as far as Miss O'Brookomore is concerned; for Mabel elopes
with the "Count," and the Biographer is plunged into such intense
misery at this treachery that Firbank devotes an entire chapter to
it. Chapter XX is, as we have already noted, composed of a total
of eight words and eight exclamation points; and all of the words
are "Mabel!" Miss Collins' scatterbrained ways are most clearly
shown in the letter of explanation she sends to Miss O'Brookomore:

Dear Gerald [her shortened form of Geraldine]—I was married
this morning and we leave tomorrow for Corfu don't worry about me
dear I'm alright O darling I'm the happiest girl in Greece I wore my
little amber tricorne cap dear and Oio gave me the violets I shall get
my trousseau bit by bit I suppose as we go along I had wanted rather
badly to be married in the Kapniaraea but it was a Registry after all
good-by now Gerald and take care of yourself dear do in haste yrs
always affectionately
                                                        Mabina Pastorelli[6]

Thus ends Part I, which is a series of fragmentary adventures
rather weakly strung together.

In Part II of *Inclinations*, which is shorter and far more unified,
the action takes place at "Bovon," the unrentable Collins home-
stead in Yorkshire. "Mabina" has returned home with an "interesting little pickle . . . [a] Roman rascal" who was "taken around"
to St. Peter's for his baptism, where he "smacked his Holiness."

The Collins family is composed of a doughty father, a rather feeble-minded sister, and Mrs. Collins, who is another Lady Bracknell. Though Mrs. Collins is not so formidable as Wilde's character, she expresses on at least two occasions ideas that are exactly like those expressed by Lady Bracknell. She forbids her daughter Daisy to learn to read and write, and is so proud of her ignorance that she often asks Daisy to "display" it for a visiting friend, and we are reminded of Lady Bracknell's famous remark: "I do not approve of anything that tampers with natural ignorance. Ignorance is like a delicate exotic fruit; touch it and the bloom is gone." On another occasion Mrs. Collins expresses her approval of someone who refuses to acquire a meadow because "Land nowadays is much too impoverishing." Lady Bracknell said of land that it has "ceased to be either a profit or a pleasure." And, like Lady Bracknell, Mrs. Collins is acutely aware of the niceties of social intercourse, though not very worried about matters of life and death. Her husband, like Lord Bracknell, has very nearly disappeared from the scene as the result of her dominance.

At Bovon there is little to do except to gossip and try to pass the time until the Count arrives from Italy. Mabel explains his absence by alluding to the "Vintage" which requires his presence. Mabel and Daisy sit in the garden and try to think of things to do:

> "Let's all lie down on the grass as if we were dead.
> "It's too hot for rough games." [7]

Mrs. Collins finally arranges an elegant dinner party which is described in the two versions, mentioned above, of Chapter IV. Finally, a letter arrives from the Count with the news that he will arrive *"Verso la sera,"* and so the novel concludes happily with Mrs. Collins laying down plans for a welcoming dinner.

Inclinations is one of Firbank's less impressive achievements because of its lack of order and because he kept to a minimum the descriptions and absurdities that enrich his other works. It is as though he felt a need to prove that he could write a real novel, with real dialogue (though, of course, dialogue full of absurdities) rather than a series of fantastic scenes which are complete in themselves but which unite to form a complete work. The result is that *Inclinations* has fewer memorable moments than the later

works do. Yet the novel is worth some close attention, for it shows
that Firbank's sense of the grotesque was already developing, and
it is a vast improvement upon *Odette*. The decade that separates
the two works was obviously one in which Firbank's literary judgment matured considerably. He wrote two novels during the period, *The Artificial Princess* and *Vainglory*. These are not dealt
with in strict chronological order because *The Artificial Princess*
probably received some revision after 1925, as I have noted; and
Vainglory is so very good that it deserves to be treated with a
group of longer and more important novels.

III   *Wilde, Strauss, Beardsley and Salome*

The Artificial Princess (which was published posthumously in
1934) is genuine Firbank. In it, his talent appears almost fully
developed, already having about it the characteristics which make
it unique. In this novella we may find the rich use of allusion (to
things actual and imagined); minute details about fashion and
landscape; the hints of homosexuality and a discreet interest in
indiscreet sex; the bits of overheard conversation; the heavy use of
simile and color images which make the novels seem, at times, like
prose representations of pre-Raphaelite paintings; the elaborate
parenthetical irrelevancies; and the absurd juxtapositions which
are the hallmarks of much of his work. One of the characters describes a painter's work in this way: "'. . . I like his pictures; they
are so exquisitely unreal . . . I admire the fantastic grandeur of
his backgrounds, his looped-back portieres, and towering storm-
clouds . . . so sweet.'" [8] And this description applies equally
well to Firbank's world in this and in the later novels: it is essentially pictorial, and it is full of elaborate Baroque detail and flow
and movement. The portieres are always looped back so that the
reader seems to be a *voyeur* and eavesdropper standing at some
unlikely window.

The Princess of the title is artificial only because she has come
to her title by her mother's second marriage and because she'd like
to be "a second Salome"—an artificial Princess of Judea. She is a
fairly typical Firbank heroine, even in her appearance: "people
either admired the Princess very much, or they didn't admire her
at all. Like a Virgin in a missal her figure lacked consequence—
sex." She is called "My tall-tall schoolboy" by her mother, and she
is "adored" by the "amiable beauties" who see her at the Casino.

She is, in short, androgynous. Her features are a compound of feminine and masculine characteristics; the result is that she appeals to both sexes, a characteristic that is common to many of Firbank's characters. We are reminded of the ladies in Beardsley's fantastic drawings, with their sensual, vividly sexual appearance which is, at the same time, grotesque and somehow unfeminine.

The perversity to which I have referred may be amply illustrated by an excerpt from the early pages of *The Artificial Princess.* The scene is, of course, taken out of context; but the nature of the story doesn't make that fact a handicap. The language, the lush and ludicrous descriptions, the references to art, the impious suggestiveness of the picture—everything, in short, is typical Firbank. This little passage might be seen as a microcosm of Firbankian perversity:

The Baroness fixed enormous eyes on a Crucifixion by a pupil of Félicien Rops—a pale woman seen stretched upon a cross in a silver tea gown, with a pink Rose in her powdered hair; the pearls about her throat bound her faster to the cross, and splendid lace draped her bleeding hands and feet. . . . For a moment the Baroness seemed lost in thought, imagining the martyred woman's lover.

'He must have been very young to be so cruel,' she told herself.
'. . . —I am wondering,' she said at length, after a pause just long enough for an Angel to pass by, flying slowly, 'what I shall wear. I hope the man [for whom she is waiting] is shy and not at all forward; think! dear, if he should molest me! I cannot forget poor Gilda's fate in that very faded opera we saw last night.'

. . . .

'Should I,' she enquired, 'wear the little gown I wore at poor Eulalia's funeral, or dare I wear a heavenly thing—Scenes from the Decameron painted upon chiffon, and an enormous sombrero with silver strings?' [9]

Cruel lovers, a weak and shy man, a weird crucifixion, an elaborate *toilette, Rigoletto,* the image of the angel—all of these are elements of Firbank's special style and manner. In his later novels he tends to write with less density of detail, and to make his details a more integral part of the scene; but here we may see an exaggerated example of his peculiar art. All of these details are "Decadent" and show the combination of the sacred and profane and the love of richness that are characteristic of the writers of that movement. Much of this sort of thing is visual—that is, we

are constantly forced to "see" the scene rather than to just imagine
it in some vague way. Aubrey Beardsley's drawings may be said to
be the "photographs" of that Decadent world.

One of Beardsley's most famous drawings is the picture of Salome in a dress made of peacock feathers. Such a picture would
have been particularly attractive to Firbank, and there is little
doubt that he saw it. Indeed, Salome and her grisly story were
very much in the air at the time Firbank was writing *The Artificial
Princess*. Not only had Beardsley drawn pictures of her, but, of
course, Oscar Wilde had written his play about her only a decade
earlier. Salome had invaded yet another art form, however, for
in 1905 Strauss had completed his opera (most people felt that
it was notorious) based on a German translation of Wilde's play.

The climax of Strauss's one-act opera is the moment when
Salome receives the head of the Prophet John the Baptist as a reward for doing the famous Dance of the Seven Veils for her step-
father's after-dinner entertainment. Salome sings a long monologue (it is not really an aria) to the head; the burden of her
monologue is that the Prophet has spurned her advances in life;
but she will now have her way with him—or, at least, with part of
him. As the discordant notes rise in volume and the mood of the
opera rises in intensity, all finally resolves in a demented version
of an ordinary aria. All of the discordant themes come together
when Salome kisses the lips of the Prophet and when she asks if
their bitter taste is that of love or of death.

The opera is one of the great triumphs of the Decadent period.[10]
Richard Strauss used music to emphasize the Impressionistic and
Decadent qualities of Wilde's play (which had been written, incidentally, in French because the sound of the language had
"quelque chose de curieux et de sensuel" about it which made it
more suitable to the subject than English would have been). To-
day, almost everyone knows *Salome*, but in 1915, Strauss's music
of the opera was still considered *avant-garde;* and, as I have
noted, the story was thought disgusting and the opera itself notorious. New York, for instance, could not stomach it in 1907; it was
dropped from the Metropolitan's repertory after only one performance, and it did not return for several decades. Firbank is,
therefore, being both *au courant* and "shocking" in using the Salome theme in his novella; and the knowledgeable reader who
knew of Wilde's play would have seen further signs of degrada-

tion in the fact that Firbank should have deliberately chosen to write about themes used by the disgraced Wilde.

Firbank takes no chances that anyone will miss the associations with Strauss. The Princess refers to herself as having a "Salomesque temperament," and she hums at one point "a certain air by Strauss." She notes that her mother "recalls Herodias," and that the King "will certainly be made into an Opera after he is dead." The man whom the Princess has chosen as *her* prophet is St. John Pellegrin; she even practices a dance of the Seven Veils: "Far off, in the Palace, the Princess, who had obtained the King's word, that she might ask, during dessert, for anything she pleased, had risen from her bath, and was dancing a Tarantella before the Mirror, in just a bracelet and a rope of pearls." [11] The bloody and decadent tale of Salome and her fatal dance is reduced by Firbank to a ludicrous scene in which, "during dessert," the gift may be demanded. Of course it isn't, for St. John turns out to be "common" and not to the Princess's liking.

There is a twist to Firbank's use of the Salome story, for he has his characters getting it confused with *Hamlet*. The Princess's mother has married her brother-in-law with unseemly haste, while the King has an "incurable habit of prodding curtains," which, says the Princess ridiculously, makes him "like Herod."

In Firbank's later work, certain devices appear with some frequency, such as bits of imaginary hagiography. In *The Artificial Princess*, we are given some of the story of St. Aurora de Vauvilliers:

  . . . Aurora who had set sail one languid summer evening with just a faithful maid and a Book of Hours . . . Aurora who, before she had been at sea a week, was captured by Pirates, and after enduring untold horrors made her escape on a loose board disguised as a man. . . . Aurora who was cast at length upon a desolate shore, where she led for five years the Simple Life. Aurora who returned at length to her own dear France, with wonderful silver hair, more captivating than she had ever been before. Aurora who became the rage, attended fashionable assemblies, and who, whilst on a round of visits to the Chateaux in Touraine, had expired quite beautifully, one All Hallows Eve at the Castle of Loches.[12]

Firbank obviously derived great pleasure from creating these capsule biographies, for his novels are full of them while *The Flower*

Beneath the Foot is the whole story of the early days of St. Laura
de Nazianzi. All of these brief lives of saints are impious and
witty—full of absurd juxtapositions and often a bit bawdy.

In later novels, too, Firbank uses ellipses and dots to indicate
either phrases that are "unspeakable" or surprise and amazement.
The device works splendidly, for it casts the burden of imagining
a pregnant silence upon the reader who will fill in the spaces with
whatever his imagination is fertile enough to create. In *The Artificial Princess* there are some primitive stabs at this technique
which was to become one of his characteristic and masterful devices.

Firbank abandoned, however, one device which he employs in
The Artificial Princess: the use of titles at the heads of chapters.
Because so much of his work is suggestive and allusive, titles are
an unnecessary addition; and he was wise to abandon these
guides to his reader's view of the novel. Chapter III of *The Artificial Princess* is entitled "Walpurgis—(Polite)," which forces the
reader to see the scenes which take place in it as a congregation of
witches engaging in a profane dance; the title is, of course, symbolic, for the witches are the "ordinary" men and women of Firbankian society; and the dance they do is not a literal one but a
polite and intricate one in which they somehow manage to keep
their balance. Firbank's device of the overheard conversation may
be quoted to show how this "dance" works and also to indicate
that he had achieved a good deal of literary maturity by this time:

> There came a babel of voices: 'Such a cat! I would, dear, if I could
> only move my poor hips.'
> 'Insolence!'
> '. . . As if I were no more than the wife of an Aide-de-camp!'
> 'Above social littleness.'
> 'Those "Isolde" cocktails make one very amorous!'
> 'Would you mind not hurting me with your fan?'
> 'Oh! Be careful there, Countess, of some horses' offal.'
> 'I hear that your wife and my wife . . . but I fancy there's
> nothing in it . . .' [13]

As Anthony Powell writes in his "Preface" to *The Complete
Works of Ronald Firbank,* "Those already familiar with his novels
need not be reminded of his extraordinary facility in giving an
impression of a crowd of people 'making conversation' in a room."

Firbank's talent for creating this sense of a crowd is his greatest achievement in depicting society. We are constantly aware of the crowd at hand, of movement and flux, and of the complexity of human relationships. There are many levels of reality, and Firbank tries to picture them all concurrently. The result is, of course, absurdity.

It is in *The Artificial Princess* that Firbank's overwhelming interest in women's dress is first clearly shown. In this novel, the dresses of the women bear no relationship to any known period or fashion; they are the incredible creations of Firbank's mind. They do not contribute to an understanding of the character's taste but are things unto themselves. The Baroness's chiffon robe, painted with scenes from the Decameron, is an example. Plenty of others are readily available: "She wore a gown neither blue nor green, like the eggshell of a thrush, and a wreath of flat silver Vine leaves fastened across her hair. In her gracile fingers, long like a bunch of ribands, she carried a bouquet of full white tulips, and slung from her waist an enormous fan of seagulls' wings."[14] Or:

Flushed to the color of a Malmaison, she was looking conspicuous in silver tissue and diamonds, her long train spread, shimmering, over the steps behind, with the exquisite restraint of a waterfall in a poem. Above, from the fortifications of a lofty tiara, an ostrich feather fluttered in her hair, as from a Citadel. What radiancy! The moths caught themselves in her crown, and beat their soft wings against the crystals in her gown; with a scream she felt their cold caress upon her throat and breast.[15]

Or: "She was arrayed in a Chinese wrapper, embroidered with Junks riding on a sea of flowers, whose foam turning to Plum-blossom, blew right in at the open doors of the Pagodas, that peeped provokingly through wisks of cloud."[16] All of these passages occur within a total of seven pages, and there are others, such as one which describes "a dainty Queen arrayed in wind-blown draperies and stone-rosettes," while another woman is "swathed in many shades of violet" and praises the "ghoulish cut [of a] skirt." Individually, some of these costumes are conceivable; but *en masse* they are only of Firbank's world, and produce a scene full of color and fantasy. His sensual delight in color and in contrasting textures is evident throughout all of the novels—and recalls the meticulously detailed canvases of Burne-Jones or Rossetti. Remnants of pre-Raphaelite taste often appear in Firbank's writing, and occasionally his characters seem to be modelled upon the women in their canvases. The Baroness Rudleib, for example, has "that faint consumptive colouring that connoisseurs so admire"; and we recall that the women in the pre-Raphaelite pictures often had "faint consumptive colouring" and that they set a fashion among some elements of mid-Victorian society.

Firbank's love of color and detail is not entirely devoted, however, to the descriptions of clothing. All of his work abounds in color, and he occasionally writes passages of great beauty. Sometimes these passages are interspersed with absurdities as in the following:

> They pulled up before a signpost, looking like a very thin Pierrot, as it pointed a white arm backwards, towards the Capital. The wind had fallen and the Roses on the hedges hung motionless on the thick blue air, as though posing for a study in Still-life for a Flower painter who had failed to come. . . . In pale stripes ran the Cuckoo-flower; in wavy lines coiled the Daises; here and there, weary with sweetness, stretched patches of ruffled clover, and once or twice, something more richly brittle—a speckled Orchid. Above, wrapped in evening haze, rose the loftier slopes like rubed-out charcoal where they touched the sky.[17]

The hothouse quality of the scene is typical of the Decadence, while the comparison of nature to art is also typical of the late nineteenth-century writers both in France and in England. Wilde uses similes that are similar to Firbank's in his *Salome* when he is describing the Prophet whose eyes are "like black holes burned by torches in a tapestry of Tyre" and whose hair is like "clusters of black grapes that hang from the vine-trees of Edom." His body is compared to a "column of ivory" (an image which is absurdly paralleled in *The Artificial Princess* in the description of the Queen who "was looking like a column in a white velvet dinner gown . . ."); and there is a constant appeal to the senses of the reader. Firbank's images are extremely sensual, but they are also grotesque.

I have said little of the plot of *The Artificial Princess* except as it relates to the Salome legend because there is so very little plot to speak about. It is simply the story of the Princess's attempts to meet with a "Prophet" who will help her to round out the role of Salome which she wishes to play in "real" life. Her accomplice is the Baroness Rudleib, who is planning to flee the court at the end of the story, because she has failed to deliver, personally, an invitation from the Princess to St. John and is sure of being found out. She had failed to deliver the invitation because she met an old lover while en route to St. John's villa. This simple plot is no more than a very small framework which Firbank uses as support for his descriptive passages and witty jokes. Events are not important in his novels; there are almost no surprises in them anywhere. Instead, the thread of a plot is little more than an excuse for the creation of a whole set of fantastic characters who live in a fantastic world.

The Artificial Princess presents Firbank's talent to us in nearly full flower. With minor modifications and refinements, his work was to be almost entirely in this vein from this point on. Just how much of *The Artificial Princess* is genuinely early is impossible to know; Firbank called it "unfinished" as late as 1925, but he had little time to revise his manuscript after that date, and it is known that he had more or less forgotten about its existence until he discovered it among some of his mother's papers. Miss Benkovitz, in her bibliography of Firbank, says: "Each of the two drafts of his unpublished preface . . . gives a different date. One says the novel was written "while preparing for the Cambridge 'Littlego': (A.D. 1906)"; the other names 1910 instead of 1906. In either case it remained unfinished until after 22 June 1925. On 22 June Firbank wrote to Van Vechten that when he sorted his mother's papers following her death in the spring he found a number of his early writings; among them he listed *The Artificial Princess*.[18] In 1925, long after Firbank had written some very fine fiction, he said of this early performance that he was "delighted" by it. It is probable, then, that at least the majority of the novel exists as it did when he first wrote it either in 1906 or in 1910. If the first date is accurate, then Firbank was only twenty years old and had published only the inferior *Odette* and *A Study in Temperament* (see Chapter 5), so that his achievement is remarkable. If *The Artificial Princess* was written in 1910, it helps to fill in a long gap of nearly a decade between *Odette* and *Vainglory*. *Vainglory* is very good, indeed, so we might conclude that *The Artificial Princess* is a kind of apprentice work which may be seen as a transition between the early, highly imitative work, and the later highly original work.

These three novels show us some of Firbank's characteristics, but they should do little more than provide a suggestion of his later achievements. *Odette* is, simply, bad, though it is significant for its shows that Firbank did have a serious side and that he was capable of moralizing seriously. It shows, too, his early feelings about religious matters, which is of great interest in the light of his later treatment of the Church in such novels as *The Flower Beneath the Foot* and *Concerning the Eccentricities of Cardinal Pirelli*. Still, its value is chiefly that of a curiosity for it is not a significant piece of Firbank's art. It is significant that the central characters in all of these earliest works are females, for almost all of his main characters were to be feminine. He must have listened with great care to the conversations around him as he sat in the cafés and drawing rooms of London; and—as the bits of conversation floated to him, full of irrelevancies and overheard intimacies—he must have made a mental record of what he heard. Indeed, he kept elaborate notebooks in which he recorded both conversation and puns for later use. Obviously, he took his writing very seriously.

CHAPTER 3

Firbank and the World of His Novels: 1914–1921

VAINGLORY was published at Firbank's own expense in 1915. Grant Richards, the publisher, has written about Firbank's appearance and personality at this time in his memoir, *Author Hunting;* and it is a disconcerting picture:

How Ronald Firbank first appeared on my horizon I cannot now recall. Did he sway and wave his fragile body up my St. Martin's Street stairs, carrying the typescript of *Vainglory* in his hand, or did he send it to me by post? I think he must have come himself, for otherwise I do not suppose I should have read far into even so slight a manuscript. I must have had some personal motive. Firbank's personality would have supplied it. His was not a figure that you could easily forget—and yet, as far as the beginning is concerned at least, I have allowed much to fade.

. . . .

But first I refused the book. Firbank came down to see me about it and undulated shyly about the room. What was the matter with his story? Surely it was better than most stories. He had attempted to do something like Beardsley had done in the illustrations to *The Rape of the Lock.* Was I an admirer of Beardsley? Did I like Felicien Rops' work? . . . Surely I would bring his child into the world. I could not be so unkind as to turn it from my door. It was my impression that the book was so slight and so unusual that there was little chance of it selling more than a few copies. Well, of course he would like it to sell, but it wouldn't matter so very much if it didn't. But it would matter to me. Yes, he supposed it would. Supposing he paid the cost of production, would that make any difference? He was not rich: really he was very poor although perhaps I didn't think so. It didn't do to look poor; besides he loved clothes. And he waved himself a little more sinuously. How much would it cost to produce his book in a small edition, but beautifully—yes, beautifully?

I felt as if I were dealing with a child.[1]

Richards' judgment of Firbank was, of course, wrong. Firbank was no child; his eccentric behavior and outrageous posing were all part of a front designed to hide an appalling inferiority complex. Richards continues:

Ronald Firbank was the most nervous man I had had dealings with, and in some ways he was both cunning and suspicious. But he had a curious wayward charm which, however, lessened even in the short period of our association. I could never be sure of his age. His face and his figure too in some way seemed, toward the end, to be going the way as did the picture of Dorian Gray. Or was it fancy on my part?

His nervousness? He had a definite reason for nervousness in those war years: he had an idea, very unlikely on the face of it, that he would be roped in for the army. A less reasonable fear was that someone with whom he was in more or less daily contact had acquired mastery over him and his soul and that if he were not careful he would be destroyed. Poor Firbank had dealings with wizards, crystal-gazers, astrologers and soothsayers, and it was an acolyte or practicioner of these sciences who in some unholy way was to finish him off. I struggled to the best of my ability with this notion. After a year or less it died down of itself, but not before he had suffered considerably. He was during that period a man who either actually or metaphorically was always looking over his shoulder lest his persecutor should steal up behind him. . . .[2]

There can be no doubt that Firbank was inclined to excesses of all kinds; he was drinking too much and, at the same time, dieting furiously. Richards records a lunch they had together at which Firbank ate only strawberries washed down with a "double cocktail" and a bottle of champagne. The "persecutor" who was stealing up behind him was a combination, I should think, of his own self-doubt and "time's winged chariot." Though he mocked society in his novels, he did not have the emotional stamina to do it when he was actually *in* society, unless his flagging will was propped up with plenty to drink. Of the passage of time he seems to have been particularly aware; he feared the loss of his good looks and the possibility of getting fat. Grant Richards' comparison of Firbank to the picture of Dorian Gray is brutal but probably accurate. The "sins" in which he indulged seem to have wreaked havoc with his looks; and Firbank, living in a world where physical attractiveness was absolutely essential, tried to stave off the realization of his physical decay with more drinking and with more and more outrageous costuming; and the inevitable result was that he only accentuated the faults he was attempting to hide.

It is true that he had to do with "wizards . . . and soothsayers," but it is unlikely that he truly believed in them. He was doubtlessly attracted to anything that was fantastic, and the fantastic front which the "Wizard" must maintain at all times must have appealed to Firbank's vivid sense of the absurd. It is possible that, in one of his more depressed periods, he began to take seriously the words of some charlatan; but there is nothing to indicate anywhere in his writing that he literally believed in the paraphernalia of the professional crooks who play upon the gullible.

Life must have been extremely difficult for Firbank, for every occasion in which he had to "perform" a role in public seems to have been a hideous torture for him. He is reported to have hidden under a table rather than face a headwaiter on one occasion; on another, when he had obtained an invitation to visit Ada Leverson, the "Sphinx" of the "yellow nineties," he dressed himself in absurd grandeur for the presentation, obviously feeling that he could not face the eminent lady without the aid of some outward show of his own significance. When it turned out that she was not at home at the appointed hour, he was decimated; he was certain that she had seen him from a window and had, consequently, decided that he was unmeetable.

Everyone who has written about him reports his nervous giggling, and his constant need for more to drink to support his spirit; the drinking resulted in more silliness, the silliness in a greater sense of insecurity which required still more to drink, and the result was a vicious circle. Firbank nearly always ended up by making a fool of himself publicly or by being so offensive to people around him that he was often sincerely loathed. Beneath the fantastic façade there dwelt, obviously, an unhappy, extremely insecure man.

An example of the horror that Firbank raised in polite breasts is again supplied by Grant Richards.

On leaving home [one] morning I had told my wife that I was lunching with Firbank and could not lunch with her, although she was to be in town. Forgetting this, she turned up at the office at one o'clock. Firbank had come to fetch me. I introduced them, and, later, went down with her to the door. Women generally do not like men with the peculiarities of manner and bearing that my novelist affected, and she was not an exception: "Your Firbank may be all the reviewers say he is, but I don't like the idea of your lunching with him. Well, it can't be helped: don't stop too long over the meal; I'll look for you on the 4.50 train." The fact that I was to walk and lunch with so strange a creature did really distress her.[3]

It is splendid to imagine the scene—the doughty lady in from the country to pick up her good husband and thrown over for Firbank whose nails were probably painted red and who swayed and smirked in front of her. Firbank must have seemed to her evil and perversion incarnate. Firbank, of course, always sensed this sort of thing; and he took his revenge in the novels when he produced ridiculous old women who live lives of marvelous excess. But his was a very gentle revenge, for most of his characters are not identifiable satires; they are ordinarily satires of types rather than of specific people.

Because reality was unpleasant, and because no one would pay any attention to his "slight" manuscripts until more than half a decade had passed after the time that Richards is writing about, Firbank retreated more and more into a world of fantasy, trying to ignore the vividly unpleasant realities of war and economic necessity. We have ambivalent feelings about the people who knew Firbank and found him so disconcerting; he *was* disconcerting and, as I've said, frequently offensive when he had been drinking; but, on the other hand, it is odd that so few allowances were made for him.

Even such trivial matters as the punctuation in his books caused trouble. Certainly, it was often unorthodox as the quotations in this book amply show. Richards tells of trying to bring him into line with phrases like "Come, this won't do you know . . ."; and we again have a vision of two worlds confronting each other—the practical world of the publisher who wants something orthodox, and the writer who has no real understanding of orthodoxy, even in matters of punctuation. As Auden says in "Under Which Lyre," "Falstaff the fool confronts forever/The prig Prince Hal." Firbank is the young Falstaffian "fool"; and Richards, earnest and well-meaning, is the old (in spirit, if not in fact) Prince Hal. "I felt about Firbank," Richards reiterates, "that like a child he could take liberties, and that I, as one of his elders, must not take them seriously." Like Richards, not many people took Firbank seriously until Carl Van Vechten took notice of his work and began to promote it in America in the 1920's. Firbank must have felt a particular bitterness in the fact that it took a foreigner to really appreciate his work, but he accepted Van Vechten's admiration and help with pleasure as we shall see when we discuss *Prancing Nigger*.

Lord Berners tells of a lady "who was one of Firbank's earliest friends" making a visit to him at Oxford to which he had retired to avoid the omnipresent evidence of the First World War in London. ". . . She would find him in such a state of nervous diffidence that he would only talk to her with his back turned and looking out of the window." [4] Lord Berners himself found conversation with Firbank equally difficult:

> Conversation with him was like playing tennis with an erratic tennis-player. You never knew in what direction his thoughts would fly. After a time a sort of technique could be acquired. It was no use, for instance, ever asking him a question, or, at all events, to expect a reasonable answer. He seemed to dread being pinned down to any positive assertion even of the most simple nature. "Where does So-and-so live?" one might ask. "Why should one live anywhere?" he would reply and go off into peals of convulsive laughter generally ending in a paroxysm of coughing. . . . One might as well attempt to record the hovering of a humming-bird or portray the opalescence of a soap-bubble. There was an intriguing irrelevance, a delightful, fantastic silliness in all he said or did. [5]

"Intriguing irrelevance" and "delightful, fantastic silliness" are to be found in all of Firbank's creations. It is the method of conversation which his characters employ, and it is evident that Firbank attempted to make the real world in the manner of his imaginary one. It is not really surprising that the ordinary world's inhabitants usually found themself unable to cope with a creature from an imaginary world.

Even the ponderous solemnity of the British Museum (to which Firbank refers, in *Vainglory*, as "the large heart of Bloomsbury") could not stifle Firbank's constant imaginative self-creation. I. K. Fletcher quotes from a friend's description of Firbank at "work" there:

> "I have seen him in the Reading Room with rows of tomes around him, keeping up an elaborate and entirely effective mockery of study.

He read one book because it was the most trivial ever written on its subject, while he pushed away the standard work with a gesture of contempt. He handled an Italian volume so that he might derive the pleasure of touch from its leather binding. Another lay open in front of him an hour or more, that he might appreciate fully the pleasant proportions of its page. This book was discarded for the solemn reason that it looked dull while that, a Greek Testament, with a jewel set in the cover, was amusing because it reminded him of the Cyclops. Such easy contempt of sober knowledge! And in that atmosphere! The effect was shattering." [6]

In this instance Firbank created an effect that must have pleased him enormously, and it must have enraged the scholarly drones around him. Even the British Museum Reading Room could provide a suitable stage upon which to play the role of the outrageous young man, just as churches, palaces, and country towns become the bigger stages upon which his characters play their roles in the novels. It would be difficult to find another writer who managed so successfully to live as fantastic a life as did the imaginary people about whom he wrote. Wilde said that life imitates art; in Firbank's case, life really did imitate art.

Fletcher's suggestion that Firbank's "hysteria" had "one of its causes in his inability to see himself in the contemporary setting" [7] is surely a sound analysis of part of Firbank's problem. Like Miniver Cheevy, "born too late," Firbank did not belong to his own period. And like Miniver he "kept on drinking" in order to escape reality. The only reality was the one which he created for the people who inhabit his pages; that is why those pages are so very full of life, color, and movement. Much of Firbank's writing is, therefore, "escape literature" as well as satire and comedy of manners. Even the comparatively insignificant three earlier novels are about improbable people in improbable places and situations. The settings are rich in color and detail in both *Odette* and *The Artificial Princess* so that one is drawn into them and away from his surroundings. Even in *Inclinations*, where setting amounts to almost nothing, the extraordinary conversation and the complexity of the relationships are enough to bring an unlikely world to life. To be taken into a kind of dream world and to live, for a moment, in a world totally unlike the "real" one is certainly one of the effects of reading escape literature. Firbank himself escaped into his world, and he takes us along with him. And these characteristics emphasize the importance of the imagination in Firbank's works. He never draws his characters or plots from real life; and, though he is occasionally satirical, we read him for the pleasure of discovering his imaginative world—not for the purpose of seeing society's customs pilloried.

I *Piety and Vanity*

The preceding anecdotes and descriptions of Firbank serve to show the state of mind that produced *Vainglory, Caprice, Valmouth* and *Santal* between 1914 and 1921. *Vainglory* came out in an attractive little volume with a frontispiece that bears no relationship to any of the characters in the novel, for it depicts an attractive girl's face in which there is no evidence of any perversity. She is smiling slightly, and her eyes are closed; the appearance is of one who is dreaming pleasantly and innocently. The women in *Vainglory* do not dream innocently. The frontispiece is merely a sign of Firbank's desire to have his book produced "beautifully."

Grant Richards says of it: "Although I say it who shouldn't, I did make a very attractive, if simple-looking, book of *Vainglory!* —but no, Rops' young woman does debar me from the use of the word 'simple!' Firbank was delighted with the result. I think now that his idea was to have a thing look very simple and unadorned and yet to be in very fact as corrupt and as depraved as art could make it. I was hardly his accomplice. Perhaps I was his dupe." [8]

Again, I think, Richards has judged Firbank wrongly. It is true that the novels are full of corruption and depravity of a refined sort, but it is impossible to think that Firbank thought that he was duping Richards or that they were accomplices in evil. Richards simply missed the point and persisted in thinking of Firbank as a child full of innocent peculiarities. In any event, since Firbank paid for the publication of the book himself, it is strange that Richards should have suspected that he was being duped. He served merely as a middleman between Firbank's manuscript and the actual book itself.

Vainglory is remarkably more complex than any of the three works that have been discussed. Its cast of characters is much larger, and most of them contribute something to the complexity of the whole picture. Firbank's love of painting, sculpture, and decoration begins to manifest itself clearly; but the descriptions of

costumes, though extremely elaborate, no longer dominate every
scene. Firbank has also developed, by this time, his amazing ability to characterize a figure in a single phrase. There is Mrs.
Shamefoot, for instance, whose vainglorious desire it is to memo-
rialize herself in a stained-glass window: "Mentally, perhaps, she
was already three parts glass." A Mr. Rienzi-Smith "lives in con-
tinual terror lest one day his wife should do something really
strange—perhaps run down Piccadilly without a hat," and "No-
body would have guessed Miss Compostella to be an actress; she
was so private-looking. . . ."

The economy with which Firbank establishes a personality is
not evident, however, in his descriptions of rooms. Lady Georgia
Blueharnis, "the Isabella d'Este of her day," for example, may be
splendidly characterized in the comparison with Isabella d'Este;
but the chief room of her townhouse requires considerably more
detail:

The room in which she found herself was a somewhat *difficult* room.
The woodwork by Pajou had been painted a dull lustreless grey,
whilst the curtains and the upholstery of the chairs were of a soft
canary-coloured silk striped with blue. Here and there, in magnificent defiance, were set tubs of deep crimson and of brilliant pink
azaleas. Above the mantelpiece was suspended a charming portrait
of Lady Georgia by Renoir. . . . In this portrait she was seen prom-
enading slowly in an economical landscape, whilst a single meagre
tree held above her head its stiff branches lightly . . . On the opposite side of the room hung a second portrait of herself with her
husband and her children—a lovely Holy Family, in the Venetian
manner, and in between, all around the room, at varying heights, in
blotches of rose and celestial blue, hung a sumptuous *Stations of the
Cross* by Tiepolo. Upon the ceiling, if one cared to look so high . . .
might be seen—quivers, torches, roses, and all the paraphernalia of
love. . . .[9]

The amount of "art" in the room and the astonishing array of colors are staggering. Firbank is juxtaposing the sacred and the profane in the room, and he is also pointing up the vanity of his
characters. The Tiepolo in "blotches of rose and celestial blue" is,
of course, absurd, as is the Renoir with the "economical landscape."

The inspiration for this sort of passage is an amalgam of many things. It is probable that this fantastic art-filled room is partially a burlesque of one of Huysmans well-stuffed, art-filled rooms, and it is also probably a burlesque (a *refined* one, of course) of the descriptive passages that one finds in the writers of the "silver-fork school," such as Bulwer-Lytton and Disraeli. In looking for the actual sources of Firbank's inspiration, we should not overlook the possibility that he had seen another writer's burlesque of such scenes, such as Thackeray's of Disraeli in *Codlingsby:*

> The carpet was of white velvet—(laid over several webs of Aubusson, Ispahan, and Axminster, so that the foot gave no more sound as it trod upon the yielding plain than the shadow which followed you)—of white velvet, painted with flowers, arabesques, and classic figures, by Sir William Ross, J. M. W. Turner, R.A., Mrs. Mee and Paul Delaroche. The edges were wrought with seed-pearls and fringed with Valenciennes lace and bullion. The walls were hung with cloth of silver, embroidered with gold figures, in ruby, amethyst, and smaragd. The drops of dew which the artificer had sprinkled on the flowers were diamonds. The hangings were overhung by pictures yet more costly. Giorgione the gorgeous, Titian the golden, Rubens the ruddy and pulpy (the Pan of Painting) . . . a few score first-class Leonardos.[10]

Firbank's writing, in tone, subject matter, and manner, bears a striking resemblance to this passage from Thackeray. The references to painters, both contemporary and classical, is typical of Firbank's manner, and the ridiculous piling up of luxuries is also typical. Furthermore, the absurdly witty descriptions of a painter's work ("Rubens the ruddy and pulpy"), modelled upon the language of the appreciative neophyte, is used by Firbank as well as by Thackeray. It is possible that Firbank came upon his technique independently, but it is also probable that he knew Thackeray's *Burlesques* and that the recollection of them served as an inspiration to him.

Thackeray's purpose in *Codlingsby* was to ridicule Disraeli's long and involved descriptive passages in which he simply was carried away by his love of luxury. But, where Disraeli and the "silver-fork" novelists intended their lush settings to delight and astonish the audience, Firbank obviously assembles everything that is fashionable and a lot that in simply shocking or improbable so that the result is a hodgepodge of fashionable incongruities.

The juxtaposition of the "paraphernalia of love" and the Tiepolo "Stations of the Cross" is a good example of camp and of Firbank's use of it. It is exquisite bad taste.

I shall deal at some length with Chapter II of *Vainglory* because it is a concentrated example of Firbank's methods and style. Almost the entire cast of the novel appears in this chapter. Mrs. Henedge, who lives "in a small house with killing stairs just off Chesham Place," is giving a party of sorts at which the *pièce de résistance* will be Professor Inglepen's reading of a newly discovered "fragment of Sappho." Mrs. Henedge (despite the Professor's admonitions to the contrary) has decorated her apartment with rambler roses and blue sweet peas, while "A buffet, too, had risen altar-like" upon which is piled "toothsome curiosities" gleaned from a "pagan cookery-book." And, "Glancing over the dinner list whilst she dressed it seemed to her that the names of her guests, in neat rotation, resembled the cast of a play. 'A comedy, with possible dynamics!' she murmured as she went downstairs." [11]

In Mrs. Henedge's phrase, Firbank has given us the key to the whole scene (and, in fact, to much of his work). The chapters of *Vainglory* are set in a widely varying number of places, so that each one is like a new scene in a comedy. That Firbank's work is theatrical is plainly obvious to any reader of the novels, but it is a special kind of theatricality; we cannot imagine these static scenes on an actual stage; but, upon an imaginary stage furnished with the trappings which Firbank suggests and which the reader imagines, each scene becomes dynamic—full of color and movement. It is part of Firbank's extraordinary achievement that very little in the way of true "action" takes place in his work; yet we come away from the novels with a strong sense of much having occurred. The technique is closer to that of the cinema than that of the stage for, when we are seated before a proscenium arch, we generally concentrate upon the character who is speaking to the exclusion of the other characters; but, in the cinema, it is possible for the camera to force our attention toward a much broader range of action, even when a single character is speaking. The recording engineer can control the sound of the crowd so that many people may be moving around with the rustles and usual noises made by people, but the sound track concentrates upon one figure at a time. On the stage, action must remain fairly limited if we are to concentrate upon a single speaker. In Firbank's writing, we often get the cinematic effect; we are aware of movement and noise elsewhere, but our attention is focused upon a single person's voice or a single incident.

Mrs. Henedge's "cast" includes Mrs. Shamefoot, Miss Compostella, Lady Georgia Blueharnis, the Rienzi-Smiths, and a dozen others. One of the guests, Claud Harvester, may very well be Firbank's picture of himself: "Many, indeed, thought him interesting. He had groped so. . . . In the end he began to suspect that what he had been seeking for all along was the theatre. He had discovered the truth in writing plays. In style—he was often called obscure, although, in reality, he was as charming as the top of an apple-tree above a wall. As a novelist he was almost successful. His books were watched for . . . but not with impatience." [12] The last remark has a gently rueful tone that probably echoes Firbank's own feelings. Harvester has written a novel called *Vaindreams*. He has also been writing plays for Miss Compostella, who, at the moment, however, is doing "some tableaux inspired from Holbein's *Dance of Death*." Miss Compostella is a thoroughly blasé professional, as we learn from a bit of overheard conversation between her and Lady Castleyard:

'But don't you hate waiting for Othello to press the pillow?' Lady Castleyard was questioning Miss Compostella.

'I should have got up and screamed or rung the bell, I'm sure I should!'

'Really? I think it's almost the only moment in the play that gives an actress an opportunity to see where are her friends,' Julia replied.[13]

One of Firbank's androgynous men appears at the party. Winsome Brookes has a "habitually dreamy way, as might one upon a beauty tour in Wales." Winsome is thinking of being rebaptized as "Rose de Tivoli" so that his name will look more attractive on a marquee. The other guests are less spectacular, perhaps, though each of them has some peculiarity of personality that makes him unique. Several of them are similar to the "humour characters" of Jacobean comedy in that they do things compulsively. Mira Thumbler, for instance, constantly dances alone; she is "a medieval-looking little thing, with peculiar pale ways, like a creature escaped through the border of violets and wild strawberries of a tapestry panel." Her appearance reminds us again of the pale "medieval-looking" ladies who figure so prominently in pre-Raphaelite paintings.

When the guests are all assembled, and the conversation begins to wane, the grand moment finally arrives when the fragment of Sappho is to be read:

And then . . . the Professor declaimed impressively the imperishable lines.

'Oh, delicious!' Lady Listless exclaimed, looking quite perplexed. 'Very charming indeed!'

'Will anyone tell me what it means,' Mrs. Thumbler queried, 'in plain English? Unfortunately, my Greek——'

'In plain English,' the Professor said with some reluctance, 'it means: "Could not" [he wagged a finger] "Could not, for the fury of her feet!"'

. . . .

'O-h!' Mrs. Thumbler seemed inclined to faint.

The Professor riveted her with his curious nut-coloured eyes.

'Could not . . .' she murmured helplessly, as though clinging to an alpenstock, and not quite sure of her guide. Below her, so to speak, were the rooftops, pots and pans: Chamonix twinkling in the snow.

'But no doubt there is a *sous-entendu?*' Monsignor Parr suspiciously enquired.

'Indeed, no!' the Professor answered. 'It is probable, indeed that Sappho did not even mean to be caustic! . . .' [14]

The enigmatic lines are compared to other Sapphic phrases to prove that they are genuine. The Professor "quotes" some other fine examples: "*With Golden Ankles,* for instance, or *Vines trailed on lofty poles,* or *With water dripped the napkin,* or *Scythian Wood* . . . or the (I fear me, spurious) *Carrying long rods, capped with the Pods of Poppies.*" In these "translations" Firbank has caught all of the awkwardness that some translators have put into their verse, and the passage recalls Housman's burlesque of a Greek tragedy.

Winsome Brookes is induced to play scenes from his new opera, *Justinian.* He begins with "the folk-song of the Paralytics," and follows it with "the *pas* of the Barefooted Nuns." This last number is compared, by Lady Listless, to "the Sugar-Plum Fairies' Dance from *Casse Noisette.*" The highpoint of Winsome's opera is "the motive of Theodora" in which the orchestra stops playing and the only sound is the movement of her dress. Firbank's opera satires are always good; he obviously knew opera and art songs well, for his parodies of them are very clever. Furthermore, he makes comic allusions to them which show a good knowledge of their complex plots. Mrs. Asp, for example, grows tired of all the performances at Mrs. Henedge's party and says that, if they go on, "I shall have my doze—like Brünnhilde." Brünnhilde, of course, is put to sleep and surrounded by the Magic Fire in one of the high points of Wagner's massive *Ring*. Mrs. Asp's simile is an example of Firbank's occasional use of the mock-heroic image.

Mrs. Shamefoot is induced to sing a song from the "extremely exalted music of the modern French school." The song is a burlesque of the sort of thing one finds in songs of Debussy: "Ah! Je suis fatiguée à mourir! . . . Tous ces hommes ne sont qu'indifférence et brutalité. Les femmes son mechantes et les heures pesantes, etc. . . ." The *chanson*, which goes on at some length, is extremely repetitious. The central theme, in addition to fatigue, is a plea to Venus to make the singer "belle éternellement," which reminds one of Massanet's *Thais*.

Mira Thumbler is asked to dance but declines:

'Oh, forgive me, please,' she exclaimed, 'but I should feel far too like . . . *you know!*'

She smiled charmingly . . .

'The daughter of Herodias?' Mrs. Henedge said. 'Nonsense! Don't be shy.'

'Anything you might ask for . . .' George Calvally murmured kindly, who was standing near.[15]

Thus, the Salome theme enters again, and is again made absurd. But the evening ends with Mira's dance, and for it she receives a chance to sit for her portrait—a head, we suppose—by George Calvally.

The cast is assembled in Chapter II, and each character is given a few lines of description which establishes him in our mind. Firbank's ability to handle a large crowd of people has appeared almost out of nowhere, for in the earlier works (and even in *Inclinations*, which is slightly later), he did not attempt to produce an extended scene in which many characters took part. Our attention was nearly always focused upon either the Princess or the Baroness in *The Artificial Princess* and upon Mabel or Geraldine in *In-*

clinations, but in *Vainglory* the scene has been widened and the cinematic, panoramic technique has begun to replace the more limited technique of traditional theater.

Winsome Brookes lives in an apartment at 13 Silvery Place with his roommate Andrew. The room in which we find them is very much like Firbank's own room at Trinity Hall, Cambridge, which may be seen in photographs included in the New Directions edition of *The New Rythum.* Both Winsome and Firbank lived in a carefully contrived clutter which surrounded the conscientious esthete. The room is a combination of the grotesque, the macabre, and the decadently *chic:* "In a litter upon the mantelpiece—some concert fixtures, a caricature of Owen Nares, an early photograph of Andrew in a surplice, a sketch of Mildenburg as Clytemnestra, an impression of Felician Litvinne in Tristan, might be seen, whilst immediately above, usually quite awry, was suspended a passionate engraving of two very thin figures wandering before a retreating sea."

In a few lines Firbank manages to include references to Richard Strauss's *Elektra* (in which Mildenburg sang Clytemnestra), Wagner's *Tristan und Isolde,* and an engraving which suggests Whistler. There is a Whistler print visible in the photograph of Firbank's Cambridge room:

Upon the piano, swathed in a scintillating shawl, rose up a modern figurine with a weary gesture, which, upon examination, was not lacking in signs that the original must almost certainly have possessed the proverbial kind heart of the black sheep. Beside it, against a stack of music, was propped a mask of Beethoven in imitation bronze, which, during the more strenuous efforts of the player, would invariably slip, giving, often, the signal for applause.

While in a corner, intriguing the eye, reposed a quantity of boards: polished yellow planks, the planks of Winsome's coffin.[16]

Firbank didn't keep a coffin in his room, and there is no mask of Beethoven in the picture; but his room is dominated by a piano, and everywhere there are busts, shawls, pillows, flowers, prints, and books. These details all combine to produce the peculiar *ambience* that seems to have been necessary to the esthetic mind.

Firbank's eclectic interest in art is always evident. When the scene of the novel shifts to the cathedral town of Ashringford, the descriptive passages are even more thoroughly packed with allusions to artists, real and imagined. Firbank is always *irreverent* when dealing with art, and in this respect he differs greatly from the art-for-art's-sake school. For example, Mrs. Shamefoot, stopping by the Ashringford Museum, finds that the museum is full of "mirrors, or their equivalents": " 'The habit of putting glass over an oil painting,' she murmured, 'makes always such a good reflection, particularly when the picture's *dark*. Many's the time I've run into the National Gallery on my way to the Savoy and tidied myself before the Virgin of the Rocks. . . .' " [17] When Mrs. Shamefoot finally does have a memorial window installed in St. Dorothy's at Ashringford, she retires to a very simple house so that sainthood may come upon her. Here "the walls are rather carpeted with pictures—There was the *Primitive,* that made the room, somehow, seem so calm. And a *Blessed Damozel*—that fat white thing. And a Giorgione, so silky and sweet. And a Parma angel . . ."

Ashringford is the home, too, of the Miss Chalfonts who constantly laugh: "Along the crooked High Street they were often to be seen, almost speechless with merriment . . ." Their minds had been deranged, it was supposed, by the fact that Rossetti had painted them, "very pale, in bunched-up dresses, playing cats-cradle in a grey primeval waste." Even Mrs. Shamefoot's memorial window in the cathedral is "entirely without reticence": "Apparently the features [remarks someone who has seen the designs] are most carefully modelled. The ennui of half the world is in her eyes—almost, as always. And she is perched upon a rather bewildering throne, in a short silver tunic, showing her ankles up to her knees." [18]

In the Ashringford scenes Firbank turns his satire upon the ecclesiastical world and upon the provinces, for the city is small and parochial, though it is being overrun by tourists to such an extent that one terrified lady observes herself being observed by "a blackamoor" who was passing through. The inhabitants of Ashringford are a varied lot. At the top of the social pyramid is the bishop, Dr. Pantry, an ineffectual little man of the sort that has become the almost standard satire of the English clergyman; he is without ideas. He is, furthermore, dominated by his proud wife, Lady Anne Pantry. On the peripheries of the palace scene are such characters as Mrs. Wookie and her daughter Kate who live in a Victorian cottage with a dining room "in the Saracen style." In the manner of such women, they spend their time in absurd enterprises, the mother in unravelling ballgowns in order to make pincushions out of them, and the daughter in collecting the numbers from the numberplates of passing automobiles. Life in Ashringford is quiet and foolish and very funny.

The church, as usual, comes in for its full share of ridicule; it is the rallying place of vanity and affectation. Firbank's bit of hagiography for this novel is in his usual vein, mocking, charming, witty and irreverent. We are told about Mrs. Cresswell, Ashringford's anchorite, and her martyrdom as depicted in some ancient tapestries:

After (à rebours) came the Martyrdom, spoken often of as 'I've had such a busy morning!' the saint's final word. A model, in every particular, of what a martyrdom should be. And indeed nothing could have been simpler, quieter, or better done. There was no squeezing, fainting, crushing or tramping. No prodding . . . The Spectators, provided each with a couch and a cup of chocolate, were there by invitation alone. Although, in the market-place (as one might see), tickets were being disposed of at a price. And in the center of all stood Mrs. Cresswell, leaning with indifference upon a crosier, inset with a humorous and somewhat scathing eye.[19]

Even a martyrdom is turned into an elegantly stylish Punch and Judy booth in Vanity Fair. Apparently even heaven is anxious to help out when vanity is involved, for Mrs. Shamefoot encounters considerable opposition to her memorial window until the cathedral is conveniently half-demolished by a bolt of lightning. Vanity is about the only sin in *Vainglory*, however, for in this novel there is less concentrated interest in sex than in any other of the major works.

But *Vainglory* ends with a tone of quiet piety as Mrs. Shamefoot goes her way to the cathedral for a "quiet half-hour." Ashringford is not really changed by the struggles of Mrs. Shamefoot and the various factions surrounding her, just as Barchester was not really changed by the forces that seemed ready to tear it apart. In both cases, the vanities and foolishness will continue. Firbank's cathedral town is really only a bit more absurd than Trollope's Barchester—but it is a lot funnier.

II　*The Ambitions of Innocence*

Firbank began writing *Caprice* while he was living in virtual seclusion in Oxford. The mood of wartime England was completely out of harmony with his personality; and, except for occasional trips to the West End for some theater and a visit to Torquay, he tried to isolate himself from the omnipresent unpleasantness of World War I. Because of his desire to escape from reality, the novels he wrote during a time of great national crisis deal with nothing more serious than the theatrical aspirations of a provincial young lady and the difficulties inherent in choosing a suitably fashionable gown.

Sarah Sinquier, the heroine of *Caprice,* is very much the center of the novel. The daughter of Canon Sinquier, she has been reared amidst the formidable respectability of ecclesiastical circles. Her single desire in the world is to escape to London and to play Juliet at a West End theater. She has realized her "dramatic gift" while "playing at being Europa with the Saunders' Fifeshire bull; flourishing flowers at it; tempting it with waving poppies; defying it to bear her away from the surrounding stagnance. . . ."[20] Naturally, her parents, who are a fine burlesque of Victorian earnestness, are against a theatrical career. Her father derives pleasure from her dramatic monologues and "recitations" in the safety of their home, but a Canon's home and the London stage are hardly compatible. Even in her father's august presence Miss Sinquier is enough carried away by one of her recitations to suggest that, to enhance it, "You need the proper movements . . . One ought really to shake one's shanks."

Through a ladylike subterfuge, Miss Sinquier escapes from the Deanery with some of the family silverware, which brings a good price in the London pawnshops. She meets several arty Londoners, including a famous actress; performs at a "Gala"; rents a theater; and gives a highly successful production of *Romeo and Juliet,* only to die the morning after her triumph in an accident with a mousetrap.

A bald outline of this sort does not do justice to the intricacies of Firbank's story, but it does show that this novel does have something that resembles a genuine plot. There is, of course, none of what one would call traditional character development; but Miss Sinquier does have identifiable origins and a real personality.

She is the classic stage-struck daughter of a country cleric, but with the usual grotesque Firbank trappings.

Caprice is of particular interest because it depicts, through Firbank's eyes, the London of the "Decadents." Though it was written after Oscar Wilde reigned at the Café Royal and at the choicest salons, there are scenes which represent London at that time. Since the whole era was, in a sense, a burlesque of itself, Firbank's depictions of the theatrical and literary world of the period do not seem to be so grotesque as do the scenes of more ordinary environments in other novels. Yet, they are handled with a fine comic touch, and Miss Sinquier's entry into the Café Royal is one of the best in all of his fiction. She has had a dreadful day trying to find her way around London, and she is almost fainting from exhaustion:

In Regent Street, she reflected, almost certainly, there must be some nice tea-shop, some cool creamery . . .

How did this do?

'The Cafe Royal!'

Miss Sinquier fluttered in.

By the door the tables all proved to be taken.

Such a noise!

Everyone seemed to be chattering, smoking, lunching, casting dice, or playing dominoes.

She advanced slowly through a veil of opal mist, feeling her way from side to side with her parasol.

It was like penetrating deeper and deeper into a bath.

She put out her hand in a swimming, groping gesture, twirling as she did so, accidentally, an old man's moustache.[21]

Among the inhabitants of the Café Royal is a "large florid man" holding forth in the midst of a group of admirers who is doubtlessly Oscar Wilde, and a boy with "the air of a wildly pretty girl" may be an image of Firbank himself (though, of course, he could not have visited the Café Royal during Wilde's time there). Miss Sinquier's mistaking the Café Royal for a "cool creamery" leads her to order, amidst that expansive Bohemianism, some tea and a currant bun—a splendid act of absurdity and juxtaposition.

Among the theatrical types who populate the pages of *Caprice*, Mr. and Mrs. Mary stand out. They are producers and actors of great reputation and are burlesques of theatrical vanity. Mrs.

Mary is known for her portrayal of " 'the wife' in Macbeth," a role in which she was "positively roguish." Mrs. Mary tests Miss Sinquier's acting abilities by having her say "Abyssinia"; and she concludes, on the basis of this examination, that she is best suited for comic roles. At a gala, during which Mr. Mary is mistakenly knighted by the King, Mrs. Mary achieves her greatest dramatic heights when she gives a "reading" of a poem from the "seductive and charming pen of Lady Violet Sleepwell." The poem, a Wordsworthian ballad gone wrong, is declaimed "quite carelessly as if it were Swinburne":

> I never *knew* James Jacock's child . . .
> I knew he *had* a child!
> The daintiest little fairy that ever a father knew.
> She was all contentment . . .
>
> Come, Judy come, the angel said,
> And took her from her little bed,
> And through the air they quickly sped
> Until they reached God's throne;
> So, there, they dressed her all in white
> They say she was a perfect sight,
> Celestial was her mien! [22]

In Mrs. Mary one sees Firbank's satire aimed at the great ladies of the theater of the last century, the absolute queens, like Bernhardt, whose great talent was often accompanied by tastelessness and vanity.

Miss Sinquier signs a lease for the Source Theater (it has a spring in the basement), and is given a party by Sir Oliver Dawtry so that she may meet the influential members of the London Bohemia and make some impression on the critics—"such high arbiters of the stage as Sylvester Fry of the *Dispatch,* Lupin Petrol of *Now,* Amethyst Valer of *Fashion,* Berenthia of *Woodfalls,* the terrible, the embittered Berenthia." Miss Sinquier attends the party "swathed in black mouseline and nursing a sheaf of calla lillies": "By the Buddha shrine, festively decked with lamps, couples were pirouetting to a nigger band, while in the vicinity of the buffet a masked adept was holding a clairaudience of a nature only to be guessed at from afar. An agile negro melody, wild rag-time with passages of almost Wesleyan hymnishness

—reminiscent of Georgia gospel-missions; the eighteenth century in the Dutch East Indies—charmed and soothed the ear." [23]

Most of the people at the party are members of an international Café Society, full of sophisticated talk and references to fashionable places, made with seeming casualness for great effect. Amethyst Valer, for instance, advises innocent Sarah about her acting career: "An actress . . . she needs a lover: a sort of husbandina, as it were . . . I always say Passion tells: *L'amour!*" She sums up a possible leading man in this way: "He has such perfect sloth. I love his lazarone-ness, his Rivadegli-Schiavone-ness . . ." Overlooking this extraordinary scene are the "pale nuns" of the adjacent Ursuline convent. "The call of the world could seldom wholly be quenched!" Firbank remarks in a typical aside.

Despite the fact that Miss Sinquier's supporting actors are a motley lot (one confused old man, Mr. Smee, is drunk and keeps declaiming scenes from Russian plays interspersed with excerpts from *The Tempest,* while Mrs. Sixsmith has gotten herself up as 'someone *Julie* met while paddling in the Adriatic'), the production of *Romeo and Juliet* is a critical triumph. After a happy perusal of the notices and while executing "a few athletic figures to shake off sleep," Sarah Sinquier falls into the mousetrap and—with a cry that blends "half-harmoniously with the London streets"—dies at the peak of her glory. Like Housman's young athlete, she is spared the misery of declining years.

Caprice ends with a chapter in which the action takes place after the death of Sarah Sinquier. Mrs. Sixsmith, a scheming businesswoman who for a commission had helped Sarah dispose of her jewels and other valuables in London, is wandering around the gardens and cloisters of the Deanery, Sarah's old home. She is anticipating a rich and profitable future among the "courtly circles of the Close." Innocence (Sarah) has been destroyed, and avarice (Mrs. Sixsmith) has survived. Firbank may have intended us to derive a moral from his novel, or he may have been depicting the world as he saw it; but it is better to forget about "messages" and think, instead, about the civilized skullduggery that will soon begin in genteel ecclesiastical circles.

Mr. Jocelyn Brooke, in his short study of Firbank,[24] suggests that *Caprice* is not so successful as it could have been because Firbank was really writing about himself in the person of Sarah Sinquier. This autobiographical note, Brooke feels, accounts for the "irritating coyness" and the "silliness" of the novel. Because Firbank's own innocence made him "an easy prey to the world's rapacity and cruelty," his "heroines reflect his own frustrated longings." It is undeniably true that Firbank didn't "belong" to the conventional world and that his physical and emotional peculiarities made life difficult for him, but it is not true that he falls into "silliness" because Sarah Sinquier is a projection of himself. The scene in the Café Royal, to cite only one example from *Caprice*, is a fine comic observation of both Sarah and the upper-Bohemians; and it shows that Firbank was clearly capable of artistic detachment from his characters. His sense of the absurd almost always dominates whatever he is writing about, and his innocent heroines are not pathetic. When Firbank is silly, he is usually so for a satirical purpose—not because he is unconsciously writing about his own frustrations and defeats.

III *Centenarians and Some Very Young People*

Valmouth, begun as soon as arrangements for the publication of *Caprice* had been made,[25] is one of Firbank's longest books; and it contains some of his choicest writing and all the usual Firbankian themes: exotic love affairs, clerical intrigue, and life among the privileged. Though the novel is comic, there is a strong sense of the "Decadent" about it that is occasionally obtrusive. The characters in *Valmouth* are mostly old, and the setting of the story is a kind of health resort on the West Coast of England. The clients restore their health and spirits by indulging in affairs with the very young local rustics, among other things, and all of them have kinks in their make-up which suggest various perversions.

The plot is extremely simple. A young heir to a great fortune, Dick Thoroughfare, shocks Valmouth and delights himself by marrying Niri-Esther, a mysterious native of the "East." Around this simple event, Firbank winds dozens of elaborate conversations of the *grande dames* of Valmouth, and a subplot about Mrs. Yäjnavalkya, who is a chiropractor and, on the side, a procuress. The Dick Thoroughfare-Niri-Esther plot is enlivened by the fact that the society of Valmouth insists upon a "proper" wedding for the couple. Though the bride is "expecting a second enfatement. . . . she's such a quick puss," the novel splendidly concludes with the moments before the wedding is to take place. The suffering mother-in-law, Mrs. Thoroughfare, goes into the Basilica to derive spiritual comfort from the "soft neurotic light" that gleams through the windows depicting the life of Saint Autonoma Meris:

Autonoma by way of prelude lolling at a mirror plein de chic, her toes on a hassock, reading a billet-doux. Autonoma with a purple heartsease, pursuing a nail-pink youth. Autonoma with four male rakes (like the little brown men of Egypt)—her hair down, holding an ostrich-fan. Autonoma in marvelous mourning and with Nile-green hair, seated like a mummy bolt upright. . . . Her growing mysticism. . . . Her moods. Her austerities. Her increasing dowdiness. Her indifference to dress. She repulses her couturier: 'Send her away!' Her founding of Sodbury. Her end.[26]

The story of Saint Autonoma has, of course, nothing to do with the Thoroughfare family; but the inclusion, repeatedly and at length, of such seemingly irrelevant detail is typical of Firbank's method in *Valmouth*. A series of almost unrelated details are combined with only vaguely related incidents, yet the reader comes away from the novel with a clear impression of Valmouth society and the Valmouth *ambience*.

Rural types rarely appear in Firbank's work. Only in *Prancing Nigger*, published in 1924, does he build a novel around characters who are neither sophisticated city-dwellers nor country gentry. In *Valmouth* there are some secondary characters, however, who show that Firbank's wit could deal with provincials as well as with wealthy society. The Tooke family is a burlesque of Hardy's rural characters, for they have the same brooding earthiness that we find in the Wessex novels. But, of course, they are exaggerations and grotesques. Young David Tooke ("Corydon") is the object of various centenarian desires. When we first see him, it is from the window of a moving carriage in which are Mrs. Hurstpierpoint, a priest, and Mrs. Thoroughfare:

. . . a voice full and flexible rose suddenly from behind a burgeoning quincunx of thorns:
   'I heard the voice of Jesus say-y-y! Yahoo, to heel. Bad dog.'
   'It's that crazy Corydon,' Mrs. Thoroughfare blinked.
   'Which, dear, crazy?' [said Mrs. Hurstpierpoint]
. . . .
   '*Meet me in glow-ry by the gate o' pearl.* Hi Douce!' the voice irrelevantly veered, as over a near meadow, barking lustily, sprang a shaggy sheep-dog. 'Hi, Douce boy? . . . Doucey! Douce!'

The Priest pulled the light merino carriage robe higher about his knees.

'How,' he addressed Mrs. Hurstpierpoint. . . . 'how if the glorious virgin required you to take this young fellow under your wing?'

. . . .

'For the sake, I presume,' she queried, 'of his soul?'

'Precisely.'

'But is he ripe?' Mrs. Thoroughfare wondered.

'Ripe?'

'I *mean*—'

There was a busy silence.[27]

In addition to "Corydon," the Tooke family is composed of Granny and a girl with the suitably rustic name of Thetis. They are all full of intensity and earthy common sense, an unlikely combination. Their farm is an ancient one for which Firbank provides a ridiculous history having to do with, among other things, the granting of rights to Thierry Monfaulcon Tooke by Henry the Eighth at the time of the dissolution of the monastic holdings. Just as Hardy's D'urbervilles had degenerated into the simple Derbyfields, so the Tookes have declined from importance to insignificance. Firbank describes the appearance of the Tooke farm in Hardyan prose:

Now in the bluey twilight as seen from the fields the barns and out-houses appeared really to be more capacious than the farm itself. With its white-washed walls and small-paned lattice windows it showed poorly enough between the two sumptuous wheat-ricks that stood reared on either side. Making their way across the long cobble bridge that spanned the Val, the cattle turned into an elm-lined lane that conducted to the farmyard gates. . . .[28]

And, just as Hardy's Tess is corrupted by the "gentry," so David Tooke is the object of a genteel lady's lust. He is natural innocence waiting for the slaughter.

Mrs. "Yaj," the earliest of Firbank's Negresses, is a wildly exotic contrast to the "patrician ladies" of Valmouth, not only in her appearance but also in the forthrightness with which she approaches life. The other women superficially conform to convention (albeit Firbankian convention), but she emphasizes her strange origins. A visit from Lady Parvula de Panzoust (who is over a hundred) to Mrs. Yaj's office elicits a description of her family: "Geographically, we're all so scattered. Von ob my brother, Djali, he in Ujiji Land. *Kra.* He a Banana-Inspector. Official. He select de virgin combs from off de tree; dat his Pash-on, dat his Cult. Other brother, Boujaja, he in Taihaiti. He a lady-killer, well-to-do-ish; he three wives, *kra;* and dose three women are my sisters-in-law. . . . De Inspector, he no marry; I don't know why!" [29] The dialect which Firbank uses in Mrs. Yaj's speeches is not always successful and tends to be of the standard sort employed in minstrel shows. Occasionally Mrs. Yaj and Niri-Esther speak their native language, which is unidentifiable. The key word in it, according to Mrs. Yaj, is *Bjopti* which means "discretion."

The suggestiveness of Mrs. Yaj's description is typical of her manner of operating. The meeting between Lady Parvula and Mrs. Yaj concludes with an "arrangement" being made by which Lady Parvula can meet David Tooke who is, she agrees, *"awfully* choice." Having once attended a costume ball as a shepherdess, she feels that she has a "strong bond with shepherds."

Firbank's irreverent attitude toward the Church is very much in evidence in *Valmouth:* in addition to the story of Saint Autonoma, we read of the protective powers of relics when a thunderstorm has frightened Mrs. Hurstpierpoint, who is alone with her maid:

'Lift the lid of the long casket—and pick me a relic,' Mrs. Hurstpierpoint enjoined, surveying apprehensively the dark clumps of wind-flogged trees upon the lawn.

'Any one in particular, 'm?' the maid enquired, slipping with obedient alacrity across the floor.

'No; but not a leg-bone, mind! A leg-bone relic somehow——' . . . .

'You used to say the toe, 'm, of the married sister of the Madonna, the one that was a restaurant pro-prietress . . . in any fracas was particularly potent.' [30]

At the Convent of Arimaethea lives Sister Ecclesia who has had imposed upon her "The Torture of Silence," which leads to terrible frustration: "Sometimes, in order to find an outlet to her pent emotions, she would go as far as to kick and to pinch, and even to dance (her hornpipes with Captain Thoroughfare were much admired at Hare), while with a broomstick she was invaluable—a very tigress—drawing blood directly."

Firbank's dialogue is complex in *Valmouth,* but it is done with

greater facility than in *Inclinations*. Here, for example, is an excerpt from a scene in which the first two speakers are Mrs. Thoroughfare and Lady Parvula de Panzoust:

> Lady Parvula plied her fan.
> 'Even at Oomanton,' she murmured, 'certain of the new hybrids
> this year are quite too perfect.'
> 'Eulalia and I often speak of the wondrous orchids at Oomanton
> Towers.'
> Lady Parvula expanded.
> 'We're very proud of a rose-lipped one,' she said, 'with a lilac
> beard.'
> 'A lilac . . . *what?*' It was Mrs. Hurstpierpoint's voice at the door.
> 'Eulalia!'
> 'Is it Sodom?' she enquired in her gruff, commanding way, com-
> ing forward into the room. . . .
> Lady Parvula tittered.
> 'Goodness, no,' she said.
> 'Because Father Mahoney won't hear of it ever *before* dessert.' [31]

The conversation rambles on and on, full of references to irrelevant matters—the snoring of a woman in the room next to Lady
Parvula's at the hotel; the "cosmic activity" of Valmouth air; and a
discussion of new relics gathered by Mrs. Thoroughfare for her
private chapel. The scene is grotesque in the extreme, for all of
the women are more than a century old (Mrs. Thoroughfare has
been painted by Ingres), though their thoughts are a combination
of unabashed sexuality and rigorous piety:

> 'Men, men! . . . "They are always there," dear, aren't they, as
> the Russians say?'
> Mrs. Hurstpierpoint repressed a grimace.
> 'Nowadays,' she murmured, 'a man . . . to me . . . somehow
> . . . oh! he is something so wildly *strange*.'
> 'Strange?'
> 'Unglimpsable.'
> 'Still, some men are ultra-womanly, and they're the kind I love!'
> Mrs. Thoroughfare chirruped.
> 'I suppose that none but those whose courage is unquestionable can
> venture to be effeminate?' Lady Parvula said, plunging a two-
> pronged fork into a 'made' dish of sugared-violets served in aspic.
> 'It may be so.'

'It was only in war-time, was it, that the Spartans were accustomed
to put on perfume, or to crimp their beards?' [32]

A moment later they are interrupted by Mrs. Hurstpierpoint's
chaplain: "Bowing her face before the stiff, proud thumb and
crooked forefinger raised to bless, Mrs. Hurstpierpoint remained a
moment as if in transport, looking with her figured veils and
fuzzed hair-wreathings, like some Byzantine peacock searching
for fleas." [33] The flickering lights of the room, the walls hung with
paintings, the reminiscences of times a generation ago, the image
of the old lady bowing before her priest—all combine into the
most grotesque scene in all of Firbank's work. Furthermore, we
learn that Mrs. Hurstpierpoint mortifies her flesh by wearing
prickly holly leaves beneath her dresses, and spikes upon her gar-
ters. A moth flies into the flaming candle; two of the women decide to make a pilgrimage across the lawns, in their bare feet, to
the estate chapel: "A hyacinthine darkness flooded the titanic ce-
dars before the house above whose immemorial crests like a sad
opal the moon was rising." There is a kind of Gothic horror to the
entire scene that is both repellent and attractive. The women are
like obscene shadows; and, as their conversation continues, the
reader sits just outside the window and plays the *voyeur*.

Even below stairs the women live in a world in which sex plays
a chief role. In her mind, Fowler, a dowdy waiting woman who
has just seen the butler's "crane-like" legs, imagines what he is
planning to do to her ". . . in the dark of his mind might he not
aspire to build with her? Swoop! Fly to church with her: make a
nest of her? Snatch at her? Bend her, break her—God knew how!
—to his passions' uses?" [34] The language and syntax here is, incredibly, very much like that in some of Gerard Manley Hopkins'
"Terrible Sonnets."

The full congregation of grotesques comes together in Chapter
VIII of *Valmouth*. The centenarians of the town gather "like so
many warlocks and witches" to celebrate the passing of another
year. The salon in which they are sitting is lit from above by an
ancient chandelier; and the place seems, says Firbank, rather like
Limbo. One after another, they make their entrances:

Leaning on the arm of a swathed tangerine figure, Mrs. Hurstpierpoint, decked in wonderful pearls like Titian's Queen of Cyprus,

trailed about beneath the mounting moon, greeting here and there a contemporary with vague cognition. She seemed in charming spirits.

"Your ladyship dribbles!" she complacently commented, shaking from the curling folds of her dress a pious leaflet, *The———of Mary,* audaciously scouting the Augustinian theory "that the Blessed Virgin conceived our Lord through the Ears." [35]

Lady Parvula sits by "on the fringe of the throng, by a marble shape of Priapus green with moss"; and Granny Tooke arrives in fine fettle but poor physical condition. "My legs gae all tapsaltee-rie," she cries. "Just hark to my joints! I'm positively tumbling to bits." A moment later she wanders down a path in the garden and madly curtsies to all of the statues lined up there. Mrs. Yaj is in attendance with Niri-Esther, whose voluptuousness arouses the lust of most of the ancient women. Even a parrot appears; it is the pet of the painter, Sir Victor Vatt. To the cacophony of creaking joints, lustful sighs, and gypsy music is added the bird's voice: ' "Dear Vatt," it cried, "he is so splendid: so o-ri-gi-nal: and exuberant; like an Italian decorator. Come, Vatt! Paint me in a greenhouse . . . in a st-oove; a little exotic! . . . Where's my bloody Brush?" ' The scene is a literal Pandemonium.

Lady Parvula's meeting with David Tooke is arranged to take place in "a sort of Moorish palace"; but, of course, David doesn't arrive. Mrs. Yaj is disgraced, but manages to convince Lady Parvula that half a loaf is better than none, and that scene ends with the ancient woman putting "one or two pretty questions" to Mrs. Yaj about the "captain of a ketch" in the harbor.

The whole novel is like a fantastic witches' carnival in which scenes of innocence are contrasted with scenes of depravity. There is even a kind of sacrifice made by Thetis Tooke who has been in love with Dick Thoroughfare but has lost him to Niri-Esther. We find her by the edge of the sea where she has gone to drown herself. She laments the hours she has spent in soaking her arms in milk in order to make them white, when, apparently, Thoroughfare would have preferred her to be black. Whether or not she does complete the act is not clear; for, just as she is about to wade into the water, Sister Ecclesia, who is given one day a year of relief from her Torture of Silence, appears on the beach in order to shriek at the gulls—an experience which she finds more intense in its relief-giving qualities than simple drawing-room conversation would be. The last we see of them is through the

eyes of a coast guardsman at a nearby lighthouse who sees the
two women wrestling below him on the beach. Perhaps the holy
sister is successful.

The wedding of Thoroughfare and Niri-Esther is grotesque. A
prima donna, Mademoiselle Carmen Colonnade, is shrieking an
absurd aria as the procession enters the church, but neither the
bride nor the groom is present. The innocent, pregnant, mysterious Niri-Esther has run into the garden to pursue a butterfly; and
the groom is, quite simply, missing. Perhaps he is, symbolically,
the butterfly his bride pursues; for it is unlikely that he will ever
return to her since he has long since indicated his deep affection
for a shipmate, Lieutenant Whorwood, who looks like "some girl
masquerading as a boy."

Perhaps innocence is its own protection, and Niri-Esther is well
out of it to have escaped her marriage amid all that perversity
and corruption. The ancient women, it must be assumed, will go
on and on. *Valmouth* is a microcosm in which all of the world's
evil has been harmlessly caught. While Firbank was living in this
microcosm, the real world was caught up in evils far less harmless
—those of war.

IV An "Eastern" Tale

There is a pause in Firbank's progress at this point. From *Vainglory* to *Valmouth* marks a period of highly successful productiv-
ity in which almost everything he wrote is artistically mature. His
style and subject matter were well established, and it is strange
that he chose at this point to abandon them. His last novel of this
period is *Santal,* which was, he said, an attempt "to rewrite
Odette in an Arab setting—a child seeking Allah. . . ." [36] This
statement explains some of the problem; Firbank is not at ease
when writing about children. His world is a very adult one; and,
when he attempted to write about children, he became sentimen-
tal and lost his sense of perspective. *Odette* was clearly a failure,
yet he was sufficiently attracted to her "innocence" to want to re-
create her in a new guise. But, just as she could not inspire him to
real creativity, so his new Odette (now a boy, rather than a young
girl) could not really inspire him.

Firbank certainly took *Santal* very seriously. He went to Tunis
to find authentic local color, and he asked his mother to send a
copy of the *Koran* in English to him; while "at Gabes he spent

much of his time on a muezzin's balcony observing Tunisian village life." [37] The hero of the novel (really, a longish short story of approximately seventy-five hundred words) is a boy "whose profound eyes . . . had vision in them." Firbank once wrote from Algeria of the *"wonderful boys"* (italics his), and it is safe to imagine that Cherif with his "proud camel-like head and visionary eyes" is an idealized amalgam of all the "wonderful" boys that Firbank had seen in Africa. In any event, we may be reasonably sure that Firbank's feelings about Cherif were touched with emotions and passions which transcend the Platonic ideal.

The extremely unattractive style of Firbank's writing in *Santal* is reminiscent of the "Eastern" tales of Disraeli and "Vathek" Beckford, and the novel often sounds like a corrupted bit of the King James Version. It is full of conscientiously exotic words which do not do much to create an atmosphere of mystery ("The glint of the minbar, tipped with pearl, told that in the East [*sic*] the sun must already be setting. Wrapped up in his haik like no thing living, the travelling marabout appeared wholly earth detached. . . ."; or, to offer one more example, "To reach the street Bab-Azoun it was necessary to cross the Souk. . . . etc., etc."). It is fair, I think, to be harsh about Firbank's failure in *Santal;* for his extraordinary sense of what was absurd worked with almost unerring accuracy in much of the rest of his fiction. Phrases of the kind quoted here are used in other novels, but as subtle contrasts introduced to heighten the absurdity of a scene.

Firbank was aware that something was wrong, for one third of the story is devoted to the conversation of some old crones which is reminiscent of the drawing-room conversations of the *grande dames* in the earlier novels. The allusions to absent "friends" in those novels and the gossipy tone of the conversation are paralleled in this section of *Santal,* but it seems labored:

'Safia, the lately repudiated wife of Abou Zazaa takes a Hammam every day!'
'She is growing so exotic.'
'They say she's in love with a peacock's feather.'
'Give me a black moustache,' Amoucha sighed, 'and two passionate legs!' [38]

This section of the story is interesting enough, but it is out of harmony with the rest of the work. A brief excerpt from a conver-

sation between Cherif, who is seeking spiritual guidance, and the
"travelling Marabout from Sfa" illustrates this quality:

> The Marabout raised beautiful half-blind eyes.
> 'Thou wouldst visit *Mecca*?' Soft as the sound of the rain upon high
> palm-leaves were the tones of his voice.
> 'It is my desire.'
> 'There are more worthy to go with than I,' the Marabout declared.
> 'I know of none.'
> 'Far away across the Sahara there is one.'
> 'His name?'
> 'Some said his name was even as the Most Merciful's . . .' And the
> old man told of a hermit dwelling in the high hills across the plains,
> thought by some to be the Prophet himself. . . . [39]

Though Firbank "mocked" the Roman Catholic Church and the
Anglican Church, he is much more reverent when he is dealing
with non-Christian religions. Unfortunately, it is the tone of
gentle mockery at which he excelled.

I have noted that *Santal* is similar to the Eastern tales of Disraeli and Beckford. There is an especial similarity between *Santal*
and Disraeli's *Alroy* in the language which the two writers employ, the deliberate touches of local color, the attempt to make the
setting authentic (Disraeli appended footnotes to his novel to
prove that the most exotic descriptions were taken from reality),
the journey through the desert which the hero makes, and the
touches of Byronic melancholy. Both Cherif and Alroy remain
brooding outsiders like Byron's Childe Harold. Cherif finds that it
is "charming" to gaze at the sky through the empty eye-sockets of
a skull and to watch the soaring of the "violet vultures" (the color
is, obviously, a Firbankian touch). We would like to believe that
Firbank was burlesquing the Oriental tale, but Cherif is so earnest, so handsome, and comes to such a bitter end that we are
forced to conclude that Firbank wished us to sympathize with his
hero and to be moved by his fate.

In the desert, bent on finding the holy prophet suggested by the
Marabout, Cherif is nearing his end; but his dream, in which a
mysterious voice had promised "the reward that faileth not" to
those "who believe and do things that are right," inspires him to
continue: "Beneath the pitiless sun all signs of life had vanished,

and in the deep of noon the hills looked to ache with light." Cherif sings a song about an Egyptian princess, and he sings the song of the pilgrims to Mecca. He finally stumbles into a valley "that seemed less hostile" and that recalls the scene of his dream. ("Alas," asks Firbank, "was the world all illusion then?") Cherif reads the Koran and is filled with "resignation." Facing the "kindling East," he commits his soul to Allah.

In fairness, it should be noted that there are readers who have liked *Santal;* an anonymous reviewer for *Newsweek* called it "a touching, symbolic gesture toward Mecca" and "a tender Persian miniature." [40] But in his next novel, published two years after *Santal,* Firbank returns to his old style and his old subjects, and with great success. The last three novels, all published between 1923 and 1926, are all good; and all of them are unmistakably Firbank. *Santal* is the last experiment with a style and milieu different from those that proved successful in *Vainglory, Inclinations, Caprice* and *Valmouth.*

In *Caprice* and *Valmouth,* written all or in part during World War I, Firbank created a brilliant many-faceted world in which innocence is usually corrupted, but a world in which innocence has a physical attractiveness that leads to its corruption. Sarah Sinquier and David Tooke deserve what they get (or nearly get), and we are left with the feeling that any loss of innocence they suffer is really not so bad after all. "Evil" is everywhere in the wartime novels, but it is attractive evil; and it is written about with wit and imagination.

Firbank told Grant Richards that *Valmouth* would be his last and best novel,[41] and he then turned to drama with *The Princess Zoubaroff* (see Chapter 5) which met with no more success or recognition than the novels. Furthermore, Firbank had suffered a personal embarrassment and a severe injury to his highly sensitive feelings when the dedication of the play, "To the Hon. Evan Morgan in Souvenir Amicale of a 'Previous Incarnation'," was noisily and nastily repudiated by its recipient.

Santal's Cherif, gentle and trusting, searching for faith and spiritual comfort, is doubtlessly a reflection of Firbank's self at this time. He was not, for once, properly detached from his subject. The period, then, from 1914 to 1921 marks a kind of spiritual low-point for Firbank personally. This period shows also, however, that Firbank had found his niche—until the events of world history and his own desire to write no more novels combined to produce the unsucessful play which, in turn, led to his going off on a new tack with *Santal;* but this novel is the last of Firbank's blunders.

CHAPTER 4

Saints and Sinners

I

BETWEEN 1922 and 1926, Firbank completed and published three novels, *The Flower Beneath the Foot* (1923), *Prancing Nigger* (1924), and *Concerning the Eccentricities of Cardinal Pirelli* (1926). The first two novels are about innocents who are injured by their contact with the indifference or maliciousness of the world, and the last tells the story of a very worldly Churchman who dies, stripped of his vain trappings, "nude and elementary . . . as Adam himself." The tone of all three novels is one of bittersweet camp, the principal characters in each are Firbankian grotesques, but all are, somehow, more human than the characters in the earlier novels. There is less straining for effect than in the earlier works, and in several cases there are extraordinary passages which show that, technically, Firbank was capable of handling the then *avant-garde* stream-of-consciousness technique.

In a letter to his mother in 1922, Firbank described *The Flower Beneath the Foot* as "vulgar, cynical & 'horrid,' but of course beautiful here and there for those that can see."[1] These words describe, however, all three of the novels; in each, we may find passages which may be labelled as "vulgar" in their subject matter. The way in which Firbank mocks the Church in *The Flower Beneath the Foot* and in *Concerning the Eccentricities of Cardinal Pirelli* makes him liable to the charge that he is cynical; and his obvious delight in the corruption of the Mouth family in *Prancing Nigger* is "horrid." Such adjectives, however, would rarely be used seriously by the reader who becomes immersed in Firbank's fictional world; for ordinary judgments about taste and morality do not apply there. The admirer of Firbank would agree however, that much of his world is "beautiful."

In these novels we find Firbank writing some of his best dialogue. Furthermore, he has created a cast of characters that is extraordinary, even for him, in its variety and in its exoticism. *The*

Flower Beneath the Foot is unholy hagiography; *Prancing Nigger*
depicts a Caribbean fall from grace; and *Concerning the Eccentricities of Cardinal Pirelli*, the history of a wayward soul. The
settings are a royal court, a tropical island, and a Spanish cathedral town, respectively. These three novels show Firbank at the
peak of his imaginative power, and each is fine enough to guaran-
tee a permanent place for him in the history of English comic
literature. Everything he wrote up to 1922 was preparation for
these three masterpieces.

II *Firbankian Hagiography*

The publication of *The Flower Beneath the Foot* was delayed
because the novel contained allusions to well-known contemporary figures, and Grant Richards seems to have had his doubts
about the advisability of permitting them to remain.[2] The edition,
when it finally appeared, was an elaborate one, with a "decoration" by C. R. W. Nevinson which depicts St. Laura, the subject of
the novel, crowned with flowers, and portraits of Firbank himself
by Wyndham Lewis and Augustus John. The idea for the novel
had come to him while he was in Tunis working on *Santal*, but the
book was actually written in a number of places, including Versailles and Florence.

The subtitle tells its own story: "Being a Record of the Early
Life of St. Laura de Nazianzi and the Times in Which She Lived."
Needless to say, the Record is exotic; but two epigraphs, both
"quoted" from St. Laura herself, seem to set a realistic tone. The
first, "Some girls are born organically good: I wasn't," prepares us
for the story of spiritual struggles in which a good nature must
contend with the wayward flesh. The second epigraph immediately tells us that this is Firbankian hagiography: "It was about
my eighteenth year that I conquered my *Ego*." All of Firbank's
characters, saints and sinners alike, have ego to contend with in
much the same way that the characters of other novelists must
contend with physical ugliness or a terrible environment. When
Firbank uses the word "Ego," it is simply another way of saying
vanity. Laura's struggle with her ego is the absurd parallel to the
legitimate saint's struggle with the temptations of the world—a
battle, in other words, to conquer the vanity of the world.

As I have said, ordinary judgments about taste and morality
may not be applied to Firbank's work, for he is not writing about

the real world. It is true that he satirizes the conventions of the real world, but it is not too much to note yet again that these characters are grotesques: their vanities are exaggerations, their aspirations are exaggerations of "real" people's aspirations, and their world is an exaggerated stage setting in which they play their parts. All of these people are like gargoyles on a cathedral. Just as the cathedral is not a typical building in a town, and the decorations which adorn it are not those we would find on other buildings, so the people that decorate Firbank's novels are not part of the ordinary world. A gargoyle on a department store is silly; on a cathedral, it is fine. A Firbank character, could he actually exist, would be silly in the ordinary world; in Valmouth, Pisuerga, or Cuna-Cuna, he is right at home. St. Laura, then, is a *real* saint in Firbank's world.

She is set upon the path to sainthood by an unhappy love affair with His Weariness, Yousef, Prince of Pisuerga. Though the Queen and most of the Court find Laura "so housemaid" and "trés gutter," the Prince insists that she saves him from cliché, a judgment so typical of Firbank himself that it could almost serve as a guide to his standards of human relationships. Laura is agile and "boyish," like most of Firbank's women; and she is not particularly saintly at the beginning of her story. She is full of gossip and subject to the pleasures of any abnormal young Firbank heroine. She plans to attend a royal *fete* where she will wear "a black gown with three blue flowers on my tummy" and dance the Pisgah Pas. The Ego which she finally overcame leads her to "pirouette interestingly before the mirror in the last stages of déshabille, and do a thousand (and one) things besides that one might otherwise lack courage for."

After a night at the fete she prays piously: "Oh! help me heaven to be decorative and to do right! Let me always look young, never more than sixteen or seventeen—at the *very* outside, and let Yousef love me—as much as I do him. And I thank you for creating such a darling, God (for he's a perfect dear), and I can't tell you how much I love him; especially when he wags it! I mean his tongue . . ." [3] These dubious sentiments, dubiously expressed, hardly lead us to expect that the heroine will end her days in the Convent of the Flaming Hood.

Though the novel is ostensibly the story of Laura's early life, it is, in reality, the story of life in one of Firbank's beautiful, iso-

lated, almost-possible countries. This is escape literature of the
highest sort, for it offers escape from the mundane life to both the
reader and the author. Pisuerga is a combination of Italy and
the South of France and London with a little bit of Arabia and
Kashmir thrown in for good measure. It is a land of constantly
blue skies beneath which the flowers always bloom, and where
the beaches seem strewn with jewels. Firbank himself tells us
that the setting is "some imaginary Vienna," but it is extremely
unlikely that any reader would find a similarity between Pisuerga
and Austria.

The explanation lies in the fact that Firbank was forming his
notions of Vienna while he was in the Sahara; the result is neither
Austria nor Africa, but Firbankland. His words about the origins
of the book are worth quoting at length: "I remember it was at
Touggourt in mid-Sahara while assisting at a sunset from the
minaret of a Mosque, that I found the Duchess of Varna's courtdress—the green of Nile water. 'Vi' and Olga's little soul-trip on
the Lake . . . suggested itself while watching two shed rose-
leaves in a Moorish fountain . . . Other elements, of course,
went towards the shading and formation of my Flower. Which
really is as much a country-buttercup as a cattleya-orchid!" [4]

The palaces and buildings of Pisuerga are Oriental in their fur-
nishings. There is a hothouse quality about them, for they are full
of plants and flowers and lush greenery which runs riot over
everything. We are reminded of the fact that Firbank was in Africa when the *Flower* was germinating; we are also reminded of
the Victorian interest in "the East," a phrase which tended to
cover anything exotic; just the word "Oriental" served that purpose too. In a typical passage, Firbank describes Her Dreaminess
the Queen reclining on Tunisian pillows, being read to by Laura
(who has picturesquely assumed the pose of a "Dying Intellectual") from a book of Victorian-sounding homilies (*"Live with an
aim, and let that aim be high!"*—italics and punctuation Firbank's), in a room which is similar to those in which such "silver-
fork" novelists as Disraeli and Bulwer-Lytton placed their characters:

It was a carved ceiled [*sic*] and rather lofty room, connected by tall
glass doors with other rooms beyond. Peering into one of these the
Countess could see reflected the 'throne,' and a little piece of broken

Chippendale brought from England, that served as a stand for a telephone, wrought in ormolu and rock-crystal, which the sun's rays at present were causing to emit a thousand playful sparks. Tapestry panels depicting the Loves of *Mejnoun and Leileh* half concealed the silver *boiseries* of the walls, while far down the room, across old rugs from Shirvan that were a marvelous wonder, showed fortuitous jardinieres filled with every kind of flowering plant.[5]

This passage, except for the absurd subject of the tapestries, could have come from any of a dozen late eightenth-century or early nineteenth-century novels, the authors of which delighted in fancy descriptions and "elegant" language. Of course, the piece of Chippendale "wrought in ormolu and rock-crystal" is a Firbank touch; but earlier novelists wrote about equally silly things in a thoroughly serious tone.

The above passage concludes with a descriptive sentence which is pure Firbank: "Between the windows were canopied recesses, denuded of their statues by the Queen's desire, 'in order that they might appear suggestive,' while through the windows themselves the Countess could catch across the forecourt of the castle, a panorama of the town below, with the State Theatre and the Garrisons, and the Houses of Parliament, and the Hospital, and the low white dome, crowned by turquoise-tinted tiles, of the Cathedral, which was known to all church-goers as *the Blue Jesus*." The Baedeker tone of the concluding clause crowns the whole scene with proper absurdity.

Firbank parodies lady novelists in the person of Mrs. Chilleywater,[6] a novelist of Pisuerga who gladly relates the plot of her latest novel:

'Delitsiosa is the wife of Marsden Didcote . . . the manager of a pawnshop in the district of Maida Vale, and in the novel he seduces the innocent seamstress, Iris Drummond, who comes in one day to redeem her petticoat . . . and when Delitsiosa, her suspicions aroused, can no longer doubt or ignore her husband's intimacy with Iris, already engaged to a lusty young farmer in Kent (some boy)— she decides to yield herself to the entreaties of her brother-in-law Percy . . . which brings about the great tussle between the two brothers on the edge of the Kentish cliffs. Iris and Delitsiosa—Iris is anticipating a babelet soon—are watching from a cornfield, where they're boiling a kettle for afternoon tea; and oh, I've such a darling description of a cornfield. I make you *feel* England!' [7]

This wild realism-cum-*sturm und drang*-cum-*King Lear* plot is,
Mrs. Chilleywater feels, "in the tradition of Fielding."

In a peculiar way, Firbank himself may be said to be "in the
tradition of Fielding," if we are willing to admit that very small
comic epics in prose, dealing with contrasts between innocence
and sophistication, and containing a broad cast of characters, and
gently but deliberately satirical, are of that tradition. There are
perverted Squire Westerns, corrupt Sophias, effeminate Tom
Joneses, and decadent Parson Adamses throughout Firbank's
work. And, like Fielding, his themes are pride and vanity. We
should, perhaps, not pursue the point; but there *is* a similarity.

Among the characters in *The Flower Beneath the Foot* is Count
Cabinet, an unrepentant sinner living with Peter Passer, a former
choirboy at the "Blue Jesus," on an island named St. Helena. Peter's position on St. Helena is not altogether equivocal. He is described as "more valet perhaps than secretary, and more errand-
boy than either"; and, we might add, he is more an opportunist
than any of these things. He, like Count Cabinet, is in disgrace,
having fled "when the Authorities of Pisuerga were making minute enquiries for sundry missing articles, from the Trésor of the
Cathedral." Firbank lists the missing articles in a footnote:

5 chasubles.
A relic-casket in lapis and diamonds, containing the Tongue of St.
    Thelma.
4¾ yards of black lace, said to have 'belonged to' the Madonna.[8]

This little list is another of those very brief passages that gives one
a concentrated bit of Firbankiana. Each item, from the relic of
St. Thelma to the black lace owned by the Madonna, indicates the
way in which Firbank satirized the Church, his interest in absurd
"fashions," and the androgynous nature of Peter Passer who has
stolen them. Although he has taken these things for their mone-
tary value, it is easy to imagine his trying on the Madonna's black
lace.

Firbank's imaginative powers were at their peak when he was
producing *The Flower Beneath the Foot,* for this novel contains,
in addition to the characters already mentioned, a fantastic cast.
The Archduchess Elizabeth is an old-fashioned humour character. Her sole aim in life is the design of handsome and functional

public conveniences, and her chief pastime is paddling in foun-
tains; she is, therefore, always entering rooms dripping wet. Queen
Thleeanhouee of the Land of Dates is visiting Pisuerga and, as the
cover squib on the New Directions paperback edition of the novel
puts it, "attempts debauch upon the English Ambassadress," Lady
Something. Lady Something, "*née* Rosa Bark (and a daughter of
the Poet)," is a social-climbing busybody who is under the impression that the local Ritz Hotel has fleas. Her announcement of
this fact is greeted by, ". . . . . . . ! . . . . ? . . . . . !
. . !!!!" Firbank is absolute master at saying a great deal by saying
nothing at all.

The Honorable "Eddy" Monteith (the quotation marks are always used in the manner of a gossipy newspaper columnist) is in
Pisuerga en route to Chedolahomor, "a *faubourg* of Sodom," to do
archaeological diggings under the sponsorship of the Queen of
Pisuerga. He is a good example of sensual, androgynous Firbankian male: "Lying amid the dissolving bath crystals while his
manservant deftly bathed him, he fell into a sort of coma, sweet
as a religious trance. Beneath the rhythmic sponge, perfumed
with *Kiki*, he was St. Sebastian, and as the water became cloudier
and the crystals evaporated amid the stream, he was Teresa . . .
and he would have been, most likely, the Blessed Virgin herself
but that the bath grew gradually cold." [9]

The Honorable "Eddy's" personality is compounded of another
element which is typical of many of Firbank's characters: an interest in flagellation. Both men and women in these novels often
indulge in this particular sexual perversion. "Eddy" is about to be
"birched" with a "tortoise-shell lorgnon," to which had been attached three threads of "cerulean floss silk," by his friend Lionel
Limpness when the scene is interrupted by the English Ambassadress. Other people are not interrupted, however; and, though we
never actually see a whipping, there are many references to them
throughout the books. Mrs. Cresswell, the saint of Ashringford in
Vainglory, had been an avid flagellationist; in fact, the street upon
which her convent stood bore the quaint "medieval" name of
Whip-Me-Whop-Me Street. In *Valmouth*, Sister Ecclesia is described as "invaluable" with a broomstick, "drawing blood directly," a virtue admired by the old women of that novel. In *The
Flower Beneath the Foot*, in addition to the delicate flogging of
"Eddy" Monteith, we hear of Sister Ursula of the Convent of the

Flaming Hood being "Scourged . . . with a heavy bunch of keys, head downwards, hanging from a bar." The "Ecclesiastical set at Court" enjoys a busy round of social events, one of which is typified by a note sent round to postpone an "occasion": " 'The Marchioness will be birched to-morrow and *not* to-day.' " All of this sadism and masochism is dealt with satirically. Only at the very end of the novel, when Laura has left the world for the Convent, does the flow of blood signify anything more significant than an innocent afternoon's entertainment; for she rips her hands against the broken glass ends on the convent wall in frustration and loneliness.

The royal family of Pisuerga is comparatively dull. The King, "who had the air of a tired pastry-cook," is troubled by illness. To his doctor he complains of "an impression of raised hats . . . nude heads" whenever he goes out onto the streets. The Queen is earnest, dedicated to good works (such as the excavation of Sodom), and occasionally able to do some "brilliant wire pulling," according to Firbank. He enjoyed writing about her surroundings and clothing more than about the Queen herself.[10] He often makes her *look* absurd. On one occasion, for instance, he remarks that "She was looking singularly French in a gold helmet and a violet Vortniansky gown."

His Weariness the Prince is a *fin de siècle* character: "Handsome to tears, his face, even when he had been a child, lacked innocence. He was of that *magnolia* order of colouring, set off by pleasantly untamed eyes, and teeth like flawless pearls." [11] This combination of effeminate beauty, innate evil, and world-weariness is reminiscent of later nineteenth-century heroes in Decadent novels.

In contrast to this royal family, King Jotifa and Queen Thleeanhouee of the Land of Dates are thoroughly exotic; and "there [is] some slight confusion among those present as to which was the gentleman and which the lady of the two." The Queen's attempted seduction of Lady Something displays her personality:

'Let us go away, by and by, my dear gazelle,' she exclaimed with a primitive smile, 'and remove our corsets and talk.'

'Unhappily Pisuerga is not the East, ma'am!' Lady Something replied.

'Never mind, my dear; we will introduce this innovation. . . .'

But the arrival of the Archduchess Elizabeth spared the Ambassadress from what might too easily have become an 'incident.' [12]

The Court of Pisuerga is filled with lesser comic characters, most of whom are introduced to us by Firbank's usual technique of allowing us to overhear them in conversation. The Countess Medusa Rappa shows her admiration of Shakespeare by praising him to the English Ambassadress: " 'Ah! How clever Shakespeare!' the Countess was saying. 'How gorgeous! How glowing! I once knew a speech from "Julia Sees Her! . . ." perhaps his greatest *oeuvre* of all. Yes! "Julia *Sees* Her" is what I like best of that great, great master.' " The English Ambassadress plied her fan. " 'Friends, Comrades, Countrymen,' she murmured, 'I used to know it myself!' " [13] And the Duchess of Cavaljos and the paddling Archduchess encounter one another at a party:

'Have you been to my new *Pipi?*' [the Archduchess] asked.
'Not yet—'
'Oh but you must!'
'I'm told it's even finer than the one at the railway station. Ah, from musing too long on that Hellenic frieze, how often I've missed my train!' the Duchess of Cavaljos murmured, with a little fat deep laugh.
'I have a heavenly idea for another—yellow tiles with thistles.
. . .'
'Your Royal Highness never repeats herself!' [14]

These excerpts suffice to show the quality of Firbank's overheard dialogue in the courtly scenes. In addition to describing them himself in the role of omniscient author, he created a comic gossip columnist, Eva Schnerb, who is a satire of " 'Eve' of the Tatler or any other of the prattling busybodies that write for the magazines." [15] She hungrily records the events of the rich and mighty for the vicarious pleasure of the insignificant; and in the following scene, in the words of the silly Eva Schnerb, Firbank sums up his view of Vanity Fair.

'Among the many balls of a brilliant season . . . none surpassed that which I witnessed at the English Embassy last night . . . Helping the hostess, I noticed Mrs. Harold Chilleywater, in an 'aesthetic' gown of flame-hued Kanitra silk edged with Armousky fur (to

possess a dear wooly Armousk as a pet is considered *chic* this season), while over her brain—an intellectual caprice, I wonder?—I
saw a tinsel bow . . . Among the late arrivals were the Duke and
Duchess of Varna—*she* all golden tissues: they came together with
Madame Wetme, who is one of the new hostesses of the season, you
know, and they say has bought the Duke of Varna's palatial townhouse in Samaden Square—'
    . . . the illustrious Eva was in unusual fettle, and only closed her
notebook towards Dawn, when the nib of her pen caught fire.[16]

The Flower Beneath the Foot deals also with another world.
We nearly lose sight of Laura de Nazianzi in the busy glitter of
the Court with its intrigues and complicated love affairs, but this
novel is her story and of "The Times in Which She Lived." As her
affair with the Prince disintegrates (he eventually contracts a
marriage with an English Princess), she turns to religion for solace in the classic progression of events attendant upon broken
dreams. She has learned, in fact, that "most of the Queen's maids,
indeed, had had experiences identical with her own. She furthermore learned . . . of his light dealings with the dancer April
Flowers":

'I thank Thee God for this *escape*,' she murmured falling to her
knees before the silver branches of a cross. 'It is terrible; for I so did
love him . . . [followed by more than *ninety* dots] . . . I fear this
complete upset has considerably aged me . . . .
. . . . But to Thee I cling . . . .
. . . . Preserve
me at all time from the toils of the wicked, and forgive him, as *I* hope
to forgive him soon.[17]

Here is another example of Firbank saying much by saying little.
    The religious types in Pisuerga are hardly less worldly than the
courtiers. We have already noted how flagellation is a popular
pastime among the "Ecclesiastical set," and the round of events is
filled out with "invitations to meet Monsignor this or 'Father' that,
who constantly were being *coaxed* from their musty sacristies and
wan-faced acolytes in the capital, in order that they might offici-
ate at Masses, Confessions and Breakfast-parties *al la four-
chette*." [18] And the Convent of the Flaming Hood is an extraordinary establishment, where the world's vanities are replaced by
more unusual vanities:

The Convent Chapel, founded by the tender enthusiasm of a
wealthy widow, the Countess d'Acunha, to perpetuate her earthly
comradeship with the beautiful Andalusian, the Dõna Dolores Baatz,
was still but thinly peopled . . .

Peering around, Laura was disappointed not to remark Sister Ursula in her habitual place, between the veiled fresco of the 'Circum-
cision' and the stoop of holy-water by the door.

Beyond an offer to 'exchange whippings' there had been a certain
coolness in the greeting with her friend . . .

.   .   .   .

Finished Mass, there was a general rush for the Refectory!

Preceded by Sister Clothilde, and followed, helter-skelter, by an
exuberant bevy of nuns, even Mother Martinez, who, being short-
sighted, would go feeling the ground with a cane, was propelled to
the measure of a hop-and-skip.[19]

In other words, the Chapel has been built by a pious Lesbian;
Sister Ursula and Laura (who is a new postulant at the Convent)
are about to indulge in sado-masochistic whippings; and all of the
nuns are more interested in their stomachs than in their souls.
Furthermore, the injunction of *"Silence"* is relaxed enough to permit "Sister Innez (an ex-Repertoire actress) [to give] some spir-
ited renderings of her chief successful parts—*Jane de Simerose,
Frou-Frou, Sappho, Cigarette. . . .*"; and she delights the nuns
by telling them, "I always sleep all day and only revive when
there's *a Man."* It is little wonder that Laura finds small spiritual
comfort in such surroundings. In the Firbankian order of things,
lonely sainthood is the only alternative. Corruption, vanity, and a
broken heart combine to produce St. Laura de Nazianzi. The novel
concludes with Laura's watching the wedding procession of the
Prince and Princess Elsie of England. Pisuergan royalty has made
a fortunate marriage, and a soul turns to Firbank's version of holiness.

Stylistically, *The Flower Beneath the Foot* has some passages
that are unusual, even for Firbank. Since *Ulysses* was published
during the same year (1922) in which Firbank completed the
novel, it is inconceivable that he did not know of Joyce's experi-
ments. In Chapter VI, in which the wading Archduchess dies of a
chill caught during one of her paddling bouts, Firbank combines
the Duchess's wandering conversation with the Latin phrases of
the Nun's prayer for the dying woman, trivial conversation of the

attendant Queen who "disliked" that another—even *in extremis*—
should absorb *all* the limelight," and the omnipresent "Angel of
Death":

> The Archduchess sighed.
> 'I want mauve sweet-peas,' she listlessly said.
> 'Her spirit soars; her thoughts are in the *Champs Elysees*,' the
> Countess exclaimed, withdrawing noiselessly to warn the milliners.
> 'Or in the garden,' the Queen reflected, returning to the window.
> And she was standing there, her eyes fixed wistfully upon the long
> ivory arms of the kneeling gardener, when the Angel of Death (who
> had sat unmoved throughout the day) arose.
> It was decided to fix a period of mourning of fourteen days for the
> late Archduchess.[20]

Later, in *Concerning the Eccentricities of Cardinel Pirelli*, Firbank uses a genuine stream-of-consciousness technique in several
chapters. In *The Flower* there are only hints of this technique and
no sustained passages in which he employs the associative flow;
but the influence of Joyce and his new techniques is visible.

Some passages of *The Flower* may be legitimately described as
Impressionistic. Chapter VII, for instance, begins with these five
phrases which set the scene: "Swans and sunlight. A little fishing-
boat with coral sails. A lake all grey and green. Beatitude intense.
Consummate calm." Though Firbank's concept of English syntax
and sentence structure is often unorthodox, we find that he generally employed the usual requisites of the sentence, subject-verb-
object, even though the verb and object were sometimes only implied through dots or exclamation marks; and phrases like these
are deliberately Impressionistic.

Some of the writing may also be called Surrealistic. Anthony
Powell had pointed out as Surrealistic in the Preface to *The Complete Ronald Firbank* a scene in *The Artificial Princess* in which
invisible demons are flying through the air above a group of girls.
In *The Flower Beneath the Foot*, there are speaking flowers:

> 'I'm glad *I'm* in a basket!'
> 'I have no water. I cannot reach the water.'
> 'Life's bound to be uncertain when you haven't got your roots!' [21]

The scene in which we see the arrival of Princess Elsie is like a
scene from a crowded Surrealistic canvas. Firbank alternates be-

tween the dark back room of a flower shop, in which "be-tarbouched boys" arrange blossoms for the fete, and the crowded street outside. As the boys bark orders to one another ("Pass me two purple pinks"—"Thy scissors, O Sidi, for the love of Muhammed"), the crowds scream with joy at the sight of the English Princess's pack of beagles. One of the beagles, it is said, is fed "daily on troublesome boys and tiresome little girls."

There are also passages quoted from Eva Schnerb's record of the brilliant day; she tells of the old ladies who climb trees for a better view, of the address of the Archbishop, and of a family of black cats crossing the road. In the musty back room, the boys' talk is full of sexual suggestiveness; when they leave, the flowers sigh and moan to one another. The noise and colorful jostling goes on unabated in the street—all is combined into a panorama full of unexpected and ironic juxtapositions. Only in the *fete* scene in *Valmouth* did Firbank create a picture which is so broad; but everything remains under control in both scenes; both are examples of the cinematic technique of which I have spoken—of the technique which forces our attention upon a minute detail in the midst of a panorama, but which does not permit us to forget that the larger scene is there even though we may be observing a single flower at the moment; and both are Surrealistic in effect.

The Surrealistic flower conversations are not all so pathetic as the one quoted above; they are full of the same snobberies and vanity as are the human conversations of Pisuerga: 'I shouldn't object to sharing the same water with him, dear [says one] . . . ordinary as he is! If *only* he wouldn't smell. . . .' Another flower remarks that it is glad to be in a basket so that it will not be thrown from a window and, consequently, "bruised underfoot by the callous crowd." There is Firbank's title; but, of course, his title really refers to the delicate Laura whose innocence is trodden upon by the callous Prince. We are pulled back and forth between the "actual" conversation of the flowers, in which the titular phrase occurs, and the metaphorical sense of the title. We are at one moment in the real world of the novel, which is actually like a dream, and in the next minute in the world of Laura's dreams which are "real." This shifting back and forth and this juxtaposition are enough to let us legitimately classify these scenes as Surrealistic.

We should certainly note that much of the writing in *The*

Flower Beneath the Foot is very fine, and that there are descriptive passages of great beauty. In the earlier novels (as in the descriptions of Ashringford Cathedral in *Vainglory,* for example), Firbank rarely described something "straight"; he always injected the element of the absurd. Perhaps his craving for the real Vienna made him write about his imaginary one with more tenderness than he had managed to summon when he wrote about England.

III   *Trouble in Eden*

When I first read *Prancing Nigger,* I scribbled in the margin after only a few pages, "The setting is paradise. They are all clothed in flowers." A reader bent on making analogies could find the Garden of Eden in Tacarigua (the name of the Caribbean island on which the story takes place), where nature provides an abundance of good things to make life easy and pleasant. The Mouth family is all innocence, but the innocence is corrupted by the desire to know more about the world than it is actually prepared to deal with. Disaster falls upon the Mouths when they leave their innocent world for the urban sophistications of Cuna-Cuna in order to "rise" in the world (a desire which is fostered by Mrs. Mouth, who is the tempted Eve). Just as "Earth felt the wound, and Nature from her seat,/Sighing through all her works, gave signs of woe/That all was lost" when Eve ate the apple, so nature seems to suffer with the Mouth family when they "fall" from their innocence; for there is a disastrous earthquake in Cuna-Cuna. The analogy should end there, however; for it is not the abstract power of evil which tempts the Mouths but the vanities of city life.

In a preface for the first American edition (1924), Carl Van Vechten tells us something of the novel's composition: "Ronald Firbank visited Havana in August, 1922. The following month found him in the British West Indies where he wrote the first sketches of *Prancing Nigger.* He completed the book in Bordighera during the ensuing winter." [22]

Firbank's peripatetic ways again played a role in the composition of a novel. Most of *Prancing Nigger* was written in tropical or semitropical surroundings, however, so that he had inspiration at hand whenever he needed it; and this factor explains why the setting of this novel is less a hodgepodge of dream kingdoms than was the setting of *The Flower Beneath the Foot*. Firbank's original title for the book was *Sorrow in Sunlight*, which, aside from its intrinsically more attractive quality, is a more accurate title than *Prancing Nigger*. Carl Van Vechten is responsible for the uglier title, which Firbank himself did not use for the first English edition, insisting upon his original, *Sorrow in Sunlight*. Van Vechten seems to have felt that *Prancing Nigger* would have greater sales appeal to an American audience than would the original title; regrettably, he seems to have been right.

Firbank was always interested in "exotic" people, whether they were the decadent exotics of the Café Royal in London or the mysterious types of "the East." Living as he did in a solidly upper-middle-class milieu during his childhood and adolescence, the attraction of people so unlike the respectable Firbanks was very strong to one of his sensibility. He was especially attracted by Negroes, but his depiction of them is naïve to the modern reader; for they are always smiling and gay, with a tendency toward loose morals and a desire to ape European ways. Such a picture in the hands of a less skillful writer could be extremely repellent, but Firbank's Negroes (and, similarly, his white people) are of another planet: it is a planet in which the vanities of this earth play a big role, but the fact remains that we never for a moment believe we are reading about real people. The problems of the downtrodden do not enter into Firbank's world, and his Negro characters are really no more exotic than his Europeans; for both races in the Firbankian world are depicted as exotics. In the case of the Negroes, Firbank has given them the forthright approach to life and morality which he himself espoused; a kind of *carpé diem* philosophy modified by some awareness of manners but by little awareness of moral laws—except as such laws are silly or extreme and, therefore, worthy of being satirized.

Much of the pleasure in this novel derives from the scenes which burlesque European ways. The inhabitants of Tacarigua are just as class-conscious as the inhabitants of London, but their class consciousness and snobbery seem harmless enough. They seem to be the simple pretensions of simple minds, and we conclude that all of the elaborate social "order" and finicky taste which we have established in our society are just as simple-minded as the doings of the Tacariguans.

One of the finest social events is the "Pearl Wedding Anniversary" of Mr. and Mrs. Mouth. Their "ebenin' at Home" is attended by all of the best elements of local "county-society":

In the road, before a tall tamarind tree, a well-spread supper board exhaled a pungent odour of fried cascadura fish, exciting the plaintive ravings of the wan pariah dogs, and the cries of a few little stark naked children engaged as guardians to keep them away. Defying an ancient and inelegant custom by which the hosts welcomed their guests by the side of the road, Mrs. Mouth had elected to remain within the precincts of the house, where, according to tradition, the bridal trophies, cowrie-shells, feathers, and a bouquet of faded orange blossom—were being displayed.

'It seem no more dan yestidday,' she was holding forth gaily over a glass of Sangaree wine, 'it seem no more dan yestidday dat I put on me maiden wreath ob arange blastams to walk wid me nigger to church."

Clad in rich-hued creepers, she was looking and feeling her best.[23]

This scene is no more grotesque than any comparable one in the other novels, and it is just as charming. It is Firbankian camp.

Even in this pleasantly innocent paradise, where vanities seem harmless as butterflies, there are some of the usual Firbankian bugaboos. We see, for example, some "loosely loin-clothed young men" dancing together at the soirée, and we hear of the "bitter banter of the belles" which results from this subdued homosexuality. And sometimes the satire tends toward the acid—as when we hear of one of the guests, "a sable negress out of Africa" who proudly vaunts her "foreign extraction" by crying "I'm Irish . . . I'm Irish, deah . . ." Yet the overall sense of gentle pleasures gently indulged is the pervading atmosphere of the novel.

Cuna-Cuna, "city of Mimosa," "City of arches," is the center of all that is most elegant in Tacariguan life; but it is a latter-day Sodom, filled with notorious bars and with all of the delights which can lead the innocent astray. This Sodom is a European city—not a city with ways indigenous to the island of Tacarigua. We see the islanders caught up by the fascination of Cuna-Cuna's evil ways; but the sinful ways picked up by the Mouth family in the city undergo a kind of change into something essentially naïve and harmless. An example is Mrs. Mouth's reaction to a Rembrandt entitled *Woman Taken in Adultery:* "the conception

of which seemed to her exaggerated and overdone, knowing full
well, from previous experience, that there need not, really, be so
much fuss. . . . Indeed, there need not be any: but to be *Taken*
like that! A couple of idiots." [24]

Firbank describes Cuna-Cuna's theaters and opera house, its
palaces and parks, and the rich exotic life that frequents these
places. Whether the scene is the opera house or the cathedral, the
tone is essentially the same; for Cuna-Cuna is a city in which "Sin"
is the major pastime of its inhabitants. The evening Promenade is
indicative of the style of the town:

Passing before the Cafe de Cuna, and a people's 'Dancing,' he
[Charlie Mouth] roamed leisurely along. Incipient Cyprians, led by
vigilant, blanched-faced queens, youths of a certain life, known as
bwam-wam bwam-wams, gaunt pariah dogs, with questing eyes, all
equally were on the prowl. Beneath the Pharoic pilasters of the
Theatre Maxine Bush a street crowd had formed before a notice described 'Important,' which informed the Public that, owing to a "tem-
porary hoarseness," the role of Miss Maxine Bush would be taken, on
that occasion, by Miss Pauline Collier. . . . Vending bags of roasted
peanuts, or sapodillas and avocado pears, insistent small boys were
importuning the throng. [25]

As this parade passes along the street, this Caribbean Sodom is
visited by the wrath of God in the form of an earthquake. The
moment provides Firbank with a chance to write a richly comic
passage in which "three stolid matrons, matrons of hoary England, evidently not without previous earthquake experience," ignore, with stiff upper lip and impeccable taste, the disaster and
use the time to discuss their taste in clothing. As shock follows
shock, we hear above the din a voice saying ". . . this little ging-
ham gown I'm wearing I made for me after a design I found in a
newspaper in my hotel." "It must have been a pretty old one,
dear—I mean the paper, of course." Firbank's dialogue is almost
always superb, and this scene of catastrophe (made even more
horrifying by the extras from the opera house who are in their
Aida costumes and who run amuck in the streets) points up his
ability to make any scene a comic masterpiece with a few well
chosen bits of speech overheard. And, again, the effect of the
scene is Surrealistic.

Everyone's difficulties in this novel arise from Mrs. Mouth's in-

satiable desire to make a place for herself in aristocratic Cunan
society. The social arbitress of Cuna-Cuna is Madame Ruiz, a typical Firbankian *grande dame*, full of frivolity and foolishness. Her
wastrel son, Vittorio Ruiz (whose initials, engraved in jewels upon
a case, "V.R.," ironically recall the "widow of Windsor"), is the
cause of Edna Mouth's downfall. That is, he establishes her in a
manner becoming to that of the mistress of the son of the city's
chief dowager. Even in this relationship, however, there is a suggestion of something childlike and innocent; for Vittorio seems
incapable of doing little more than smiling at Edna and calling
her "Beautiful kid." There is certainly no hint of the demimon-
daine that one finds in other novels, and Edna remains as blush-
ingly frank and forthright as she had been before her time in the
evil city. Vittorio is rake enough to think where he looks at her as
she laughs and smiles that she has "not the brains, poor child, to
keep a man, forever. Heighho." Doubtlessly Edna's days with the
heir are numbered, but it is impossible to think that this would
suggest a long and melancholy decline for Edna. Smiling and giggling, she will bumble through; and native innocence will protect
her from worldly evil.

Firbank is obviously intrigued with the exotic aspects of Caribbean life, just as he had been equally intrigued by the more mundane European capitals. The rich color and brilliance of the more
exotic tropical setting seems, as I have noted, more realistic. Firbank shows us the city in much the same way that a travel folder
might:

Sauntering leisurely through the cool, mimosa-shaded streets, he [the
character is Charlie Mouth] approached, as he guessed, the Presi-
dency. A score of shoeblacks lolled at cards and gossip before its
gilded pales. . . . Public gardens, brilliant with sarracenias, lay just
beyond the palace, where a music pavillion, surrounded by palms and
rocking-chairs, appeared a favorite and much-frequented resort; from
here he observed the Cunan bay strewn with sloops and white-sailed
yachts asleep upon the tide. Strolling on, he found himself in the busy
vicinity of the Market. . . . Pursued by a confusion of voices, he
threaded his way deftly down an alley dressed with booths. Pome-
granates, some open with their crimson seeds displayed, banana-
combs, and big, veined watermelons lay heaped on every side.[26]

At other times the richness of the tropical scene seems to have
filled Firbank with intense pleasure, for he lingers over its beau-

ties in a manner which he usually reserved for the description of a dress or a hat. When Charlie Mouth is thrown to the ground during the earthquake, he thinks he's in heaven: "When he raised his face it was towards a sky all primrose and silverpink. Sunk deep in his dew-laved bower, it was sweet to behold the light. Above him great spikes of blossom were stirring in the idle wind, while birds were chattering voluntaries among the palms." It sounds like the Garden of Eden. Before the Mouths come to Cuna-Cuna they dress themselves in aprons of flowers. In these scenes we again see Firbank's longing for escape from the unpleasant reality of postwar Europe. The characters are Noble Savages who cannot really be corrupted by the pastimes of decadent Europe, for these characters *naturally* indulge in them without a sense of shame or guilt.

The snubs and bruises which characters receive in society in the other Firbank novels are dealt with in an exemplary fashion in *Prancing Nigger*. When Mrs. Mouth disputes a chair at a gala with the Duchess of Wellclose, she settles the matter nicely with a *sotto voce* remark that ends the situation: "From de complexion dat female hab, she look as doh she bin boling bananas." The party ends in a mild tragedy when Edna elopes with Vittorio, but Mrs. Mouth, with her native good sense, is willing to conclude that well enough should be let alone. Mild tragedies do not dismay the Mouths, for they are eminently adaptable to unusual situations; and their careless attendance to general standards of moral conduct (of which Firbank surely did not approve) eases situations for them that would have been painful for people who lived by a more rigid moral code. They are happy children of nature.

Not everything during the stay in Cuna-Cuna brings joy to the Mouth family; while they are there, there is an earthquake; and, though it does no harm to any of them in the city, Miami's lover, Bamboo, is swamped at sea and eaten by a shark. Mrs. Mouth is philosophical about it, however, and offers solace to her daughter with these words: "Dat death was on de cards my deah, an' dair is no mistakin' de fac; an' as de shark is a rapid feeder it all ober sooner dan wid de crocodile, which is some consolation for dose dat remain to mourn." But Miami is inconsolable; and at the end of the book she is, apparently, about to go the way of St. Laura de Nazianzi, for she is fervently involved in a great religious procession and fails to recognize her sister Edna whose fortunes, thanks to Vittorio Ruiz, have provided her with a splendid balcony from which to view the scene. Young Charlie Mouth comes to another kind of Firbankian end, "having joined the Promenade of a notorious Bar with its bright particular galaxy of boys."

Not everything is resolved, for Mrs. Mouth is still hopeful of breaking into Society, though she envies the financial success of her sister who has become a courtesan; and we are left to imagine her later triumphs. Her husband, whom she always calls "Prancing Nigger," is a reasonable sort: he is much inclined to take his siesta and let the world go its way. Whenever Mrs. Mouth begins to outline some grandiose plan, he listens silently until she demands an answer. It is always the same: "Ah'm thinkin'," but it always means "I'm sleeping."

Mr. and Mrs. Mouth are a satire of the well-meaning matriarch and the weak-willed father who appear now and then in Victorian novels. She has a strong sense of propriety—and an even stronger sense of expediency; and her judgments about the value of certain of her friends are always penetrating. Like a good Victorian mother, she wants the best for her daughters, her "filles"; and she is willing to go to fairly great lengths to get "the best" for them. Coincidentally, she will consolidate her own position as a future leader of society. Her frustrations could be pathetic, but Firbank rarely allows pathos to enter into her story.

All in all, *Prancing Nigger* is one of Firbank's most enjoyable books. As Carl Van Vechten notes in his preface, Firbank "does not satirize things he hates. He flits airily about, arranging with skilful fingers the things he loves." This remark is doubtlessly true, except when Firbank is satirizing the state of mind which Shaw's Alfred Doolittle called "middle-class morality." The Mouth family struggles through, and it is obvious that Firbank loves them. Their Garden of Eden may be full of serpents, but they survive.

IV   *The Fall*

Concerning the Eccentricities of Cardinal Pirelli was Firbank's last complete novel. Apparently all of it was written during various sojourns in Rome, but it had been conceived in Spain at the end of 1923 and the setting is Spain. It is, in many ways, a fine climax to Firbank's career, for it is his wittiest and subtlest novel, and also the one in which one senses the least strain; almost all of the "jokes" come off well, and the intricacy of the language and allusions is remarkable. It is short (less than thirty thousand words), and very nicely constructed. The titular hero is a cleric of impeccable taste and noble intentions, who, nevertheless, finds himself christening a week-old police dog in the opening scene; cruising the streets of the town in a skirt; and, finally, coming to his end as the result of a chase in which the object of pursuit is a little boy (a "Chicklet," as the Cardinal calls him).

In addition to the Cardinal, there is a fine cast of secondary characters, all in the best tradition of Firbank's work. There is a scene with the Pope in Rome, and there are the usual Firbankian old women full of gossip and lust for the young. The central issue in the life of each character (except for the Pope) is sex of one sort or another. Most of the overheard bits of gossip and many of the actual scenes are sexual in theme or content. Innocence is nonexistent; chastity, unknown. The lust of the old is matched by the wiliness of the young, who know how to make a good thing out of the passions of the clergy and the nobility.

The technical proficiency which Firbank shows in The *Eccentricities of Cardinal Pirelli* is of the highest order. One chapter, in fact, may be compared with the achievement of Joyce. Though Firbank's stream-of-consciousness writing is not so dense as Joyce's, Chapter VI of this novel shows his use of the "associative flow" and the real discipline which he employs in handling this potentially difficult technique. This chapter also contains all of Firbank's special qualities: the rambling allusiveness, the occasionally gossipy tone of the prose, the juxtaposition of the sacred and the profane, the interest in sex, and the witty characterization of the old lady who is the central figure. Madame Poco is a member of the Cardinal's household who is also in the pay of the Pope in order that she may relate the Cardinal's "eccentricities" directly to the Vatican. The entire Chapter VI follows:

Repairing the vast armholes of a chasuble, Madame Poco, the venerable Superintendent-of-the-Palace, considered, as she worked, the social status of a Spy. It was not without a fleeting qualm that she had crossed the borderland that divides mere curiosity from professional vigilance, but having succumbed to the profitable proposals of certain monsignori, she had grown as keen on her quarry as a tigress on the track.

'It's a wearing life you're leading me, Don Alvaro; but I'll have you,' she murmured, singling out a thread.

For indeed the Higher-curiosity is inexorably exacting, encroaching, all too often, on the hours of slumber and rest.

'It's not the door-listening,' she decided, 'so much as the garden, and, when he goes awenching, the Calle Nabuchodonosor.'

She was seated by an open window, commanding the patio and the gate.

'*Vamos, vamos!*' Madame Poco sighed, her thoughts straying to the pontifical supremacy of Tertius II, for already she was the Pope's Poco, his devoted Phoebe, his own true girl: 'I'm true blue, dear. True blue.'

Forgetful of her needle, she peered interestedly on her image in a mirror on the neighbouring wall. It was a sensation of pleasant novelty to feel between her skull and her mantilla the notes of the first installment of her bribe.

'Earned, every *perra gorda*, earned!' she exclaimed, rising and pirouetting in elation before the glass.

Since becoming the courted favourite of the chapter, she had taken to strutting-and-languishing in private before her mirror, improvising occult dance-steps, semi-sacred in character, modelled on those of Felix Ganay at White Easter, all in the flowery Spring. Ceremonial poses such as may be observed in storied-windows and olden *pietas* in churches (Dalilaesque, or Shulamitish, as the case might be) were her especial delight, and from these had been evolved an eerie 'Dance of Indictment.'

Finger rigid, she would advance ominously with slow, Salomé-like liftings of the knees upon a phantom Cardinal: 'And thus I accuse thee!' or 'I denounce thee, Don Alvaro, for,' etc.

'*Dalila!* You old sly gooseberry,' she chuckled, gloating on herself in the greenish-spotted depth of a tall, time-corroded glass.

Punch and the late hours had left their mark.

"All this Porto and stuff to keep awake make a woman liverish,' she commented, examining critically her tongue.

It was a Sunday evening of *corrida*, towards the Feast of Corpus and through the wide-open window came the near sound of bells.

Madame Poco crossed and recrossed her breast.

They were ringing 'Paula,' a bell which, tradition said, had fused into its metal one of the thirty pieces of silver received by the Iscariot for the betrayal of Christ.

'They seem to have asked small fees in those days,' she reflected, continuing her work.

It was her resolution to divide her reward between masses for herself and the repose and 'release' (from Purgatory) of her husband's soul, while anything over should be laid out on finery for a favourite niece, the little Leonora, away in the far Americas.

Madame Poco plied pensively her needle.

She was growing increasingly conscious of the physical demands made by the Higher-curiosity upon a constitution already considerably far-through, and the need of an auxiliary caused her to regret her niece. More than once, indeed, she had been near the point of asking Charlotte Chiemsee, the maid of the Duchess of Vizeu, to assist her. It was Charlotte who had set the duchess's bed-veils on fire while attempting to nip a romance.

But alone and unaided it was astonishing the evidence Madame Poco had gained, and she smiled, as she sewed, at the recollection of her latest capture—the handkerchief of Luna Sainz.

'These hennaed heifers that come to confess! . . .' she scoffed sceptically. For Madame Poco had some experience of men—those brown humbugs (so delicious in tenderness)—in her time. 'Poor soul! He had the prettiest teeth . . .' she murmured, visualising forlornly her husband's face. He had been coachman for many years to the sainted Countess of Triana, and he would tell the story of the pious countess and the vermin she had turned to flowers of flame while foraging one day among some sacks before a second-hand-clothes shop. It was she, too, who, on another occasion, had changed a handful of marsh-slush into fine slabs of chocolate, each slab engraved with the insignia of a Countess and the sign of the Cross.

'Still, she didn't change *him*, though!' Madame Poco reflected dryly, lifting the lid to her work-box.

Concealed among its contents was a copy of the gay and curious *Memoirs of Mlle. Emma Crunch*, so famous as 'Cora Pearl';—a confiscated bedside-book once belonging to the Cardinal-Archbishop.

'Ps! ps!' she purred, feeling amorously for her scissors beneath the sumptuous oddments of old church velvet and brocade that she loved to ruffle and ruck.

'Ps.'

She had been freshening a little the chasuble worn last by his Eminence at the baptism of the blue-eyed police-pup of the Duquesa Dun Eden, which bore still the primrose trace of an innocent insult.

'A disgraceful business altogether,' Madame Poco sighed.

Not everyone knew the dog was christened in *white menthe*. . . .

'Sticky stuff,' she brooded: 'and a liqueur I never cared for! It takes a lot to beat aniseed brandy; when it's old. Manzanilla runs it close; but it's odd how a glass or two turns me muzzy.'

She remained a moment lost in idle reverie before the brilliant embroideries in her basket. Bits of choice beflowered brocade, multi-tinted, inimitably faded silks of the epoca of Theresa de Ahumada, exquisite tatters, telling of the Basilica's noble past, it gladdened the

eyes to gaze on. What garden of Granada could show a pink to
match that rose, or what sky show a blue as tenderly serene as that
azure of the Saint Virgin?

'*Vamos*,' she exclaimed, rising: 'it's time I took a toddle to know
what he's about.'

She had last seen the Cardinal coming from the orange orchard
with a dancing-boy and Father Fadrique, who had a mark on his
cheek left by a woman's fan.

Her mind still dwelling on men (those divine humbugs), Madame
Poco stepped outside.

Traversing a white-walled corridor, with the chasuble on her arm,
her silhouette, illumined by the splendour of the evening sun, all but
caused her to start.

It was in a wing built in the troublous reign of Alfonso the Andro-
gyne that the vestments were kept. Whisking by a decayed and
ancient painting, representing 'Beelzebub' at Home, she passed slowly
through a little closet supposed to be frequented by the ghosts of
evil persons long since dead. Just off it was the vestry, gay with blue
azulejos tiles of an admirable lustre.

They were sounding Matteo now, a little bell with a passionate
voice.

'The pet!' Madame Poco paused to listen. She had her 'favourites'
among the bells, and Matteo was one of them. Passiaflora, too—but
Anna, a light slithery bell, 'like a housemaid in hysterics,' offended her
ear by lack of tone; Sebastian, a complaining excitable bell, was
scarcely better,—'a fretful lover?' She preferred old 'Wanda' the
Death-bell, a trifle monotonous, and fanatical perhaps, but 'interesting,' and opening up vistas to varied thought and speculation.

Lifting a rosary from a linen-chest, Madame Poco laid the chasuble
within. It was towards this season she would usually renew the bags
of bergamot among the Primate's robes.

'This espionage sets a woman all behindhand,' she commented to
Tobit, the vestry cat.

Black as the Evil One, perched upon a Confessional's ledge, cleans-
ing its belly, the sleek thing sat.

It was the 'ledge of forgotten fans,' where privileged Penitents
would bring their tales of vanity, infidelity and uncharitableness to the
Cardinal once a week.

'Directing half-a-dozen duchesses must be frequently a strain!'
Madame Poco deliberated, picking up a discarded mitre and trying it
absently on.

With a plume at the side or a cluster of balls, it would make quite
a striking toque, she decided, casting a fluttered glance on the male

effigy of a pale-faced member of the Quesada family, hewn in marble by the door.

"*Caramba!* I thought it was the Cardinal; it gave me quite a turn,' she murmured, pursuing lightly her way.

Being a Sunday evening of corrida, it was probable the Cardinal had mounted to his aerie, to enjoy the glimpse of Beauty returning from the fight.

Oh, mandolines of the South, warm throats, and winged songs, winging . . .

Following a darkened corridor with lofty windows closely barred, Madame Poco gained an ambulatory, terminated by a fresco of Our Lady, ascending to heaven in a fury of paint.

'These damp flags'll be the death of me,' she complained, talking with herself, turning towards the garden.

Already the blue pushing shadows were beguiling from the shelter of the cloister eaves the rueful owls. A few flitter-mice, too, were revolving around the long apricot chimneys of the Palace, that, towards sunset, looked like the enchanted castle of some sleeping Princess.

'Bits of pests,' she crooned, taking a neglected alley of old baytree laurels, presided over by a plashing fountain comprised of a Cupid sneezing. Wary of mole-hills and treacherous roots, she roamed along, preceded by the floating whiteness of a Persian peacock, mistrustful of the intentions of a Goat-sucker owl. Rounding a sequestered garden set, beneath an aged cypress, the bark all scented knots, Madame Poco halted.

Kneeling before an altar raised to the cult of Our Lady of Dew, Cardinal Pirelli was plunged in prayer.

'Salve. Salve, Regina. . . .' Above the tree-tops a bird was singing.[27]

The scene takes place chiefly "in the mind" of Madame Poco, though there are several intrusions of the omniscient author. Our view of things is, however, definitely controlled by Madame Poco; and it is her judgment about incidents that we accept. Firbank often writes, as we have seen, as though he were a gossipy newspaper columnist; but here he has sublimated that device almost entirely to the characterization of Madame Poco. The paragraphs are short, each one marking a shift of the old woman's mind from the present to the past or even to the future. Firbank combines Madame Poco's present deceit with recollections of her past ("those brown humbugs"), and with her pious reveries, against

which he ironically contrasts the "eerie 'Dance of Indictment'"
and her senile pleasure at the sound of the bells.

Even the bells perform a role beyond that of mere sound, for
they lead Madame Poco into speculation about the betrayal of
Christ, and her scornful remark about "small fees" comes as a su-
perbly ironic phrase only a moment after we have learned that the
bell that is ringing contains a piece of the silver Judas received for
the betrayal of Christ. All of these could be little more than the
mad wanderings of an old woman's mind, another Surrealistic
scene which shifts from the real world into the world of nightmare
without clear boundaries set between the two; but Firbank here
constantly reminds us that we are not in a dream, for he inserts
details to remind us, such as a brief reference to the lustful Cardinal's practice of viewing the town beauties coming home from the
bullfights.

Madame Poco herself forgets her business for a moment and
tries on "a discarded mitre." As she does so, she imagines how it
might make a fashionable hat with the addition of a bit of decoration ("a plume at the side and a cluster of balls"), and then we
are instantly thrown back into the basic plot of the spy pursuing
the Cardinal when the old woman mistakes a marble effigy for the
Cardinal himself.

Ironically juxtaposed upon this basic plot is the reference to the
urine-stained chasuble ("the primrose trace of an innocent insult") worn by the Cardinal at the baptism of the dog, which
opens the novel. The christening liquor, *white menthe*, leads the
old lady into the momentary evaluation of her favorite liquors.
The black cat moves stealthily through the room, the bells ring
outside, the old woman's mind wanders, sudden flashes of reality
intrude themselves, and an irrelevant but evocative phrase ("Oh,
mandolines of the South, warm throats, and winged songs, winging . . .") are apparently thrown together, but they produce a
complete scene full of detail and life.

This scene is very much like the dinner-table one in Virginia
Woolf's *To the Lighthouse* where Mrs. Ramsay controls the conversation of her guests while, at the same time, reflecting upon her
own past and the nature of reality. There is a similarity, too, with
some of the scenes in *Mrs. Dalloway* where the intrusion of the
sound of the bells of London ties together the apparently dissimi-
lar worlds of Mrs. Dalloway and Septimus Smith. While Firbank's

scene is grotesque, and Madame Poco is like some witch creeping about the Palace with her familiar, the effect is comic; but it is also "realistic." Out of these diverse elements, many of them fantastic and all of them silly, Firbank has created a many-layered world. The chapter is short, but it is a real piece of stream-of-consciousness writing from a time when that technique was still comparatively unknown in England. It is interesting, if fruitless, to speculate upon what Firbank might have achieved in this medium if he had lived.

The many references to art in this chapter are typical of the whole novel. Firbank had, in all of his books, alluded to pictures frequently, and had often used them as ironic counterpoints to the scene going on in front of them, or had simply created absurd subjects to heighten the over-all absurdity of a scene. In *Concerning the Eccentricities of Cardinal Pirelli*, there is an unusually high number of these allusions to paintings. As she ambles about, Madame Poco comes upon typical Firbankian pictures: "Our Lady, ascending to Heaven in a fury of paint" and "an ancient painting, representing 'Beelzebub' at Home." Later, the Cardinal is surrounded by "flapping Zurburans"; and at another time we hear of a picture of the Magdalen "waylaying Our Lord." Firbank had a fine talent for interpolating these splendidly incongruous and ironic descriptive titles in all of his novels, but they are used with unusual ironic effect in this very late work. He was, obviously, a man who haunted art galleries and enjoyed what he saw in them. The perusal of any major collection will show us pictures only slightly less ludicrous than those depicted in his works; it is just that we view them reverently as "things" meant for galleries; Firbank uses them as part of the furniture to be found in his unique world. Just as the Church, marriage, or chastity is used ironically, so is "art" used to show the absurdity of man.

Firbank is just as cavalier in his treatment of "History." One of the finest pieces of wit in the novel is a splendid "disclosure" of a snippet of fabricated history. It seems that the pious and stolid Queen Victoria, under a pseudonym, was involved in correspondence with the Popes of Rome; and her influence is mused upon by Pope Teritius II in this novel. The reader familiar with Queen Victoria's published diaries will find that the style is accurate. The result is a brilliant stroke of wit:

It had been a day distinguished by innumerable Audiences . . .
Certainly the increasing numbers of English were decidedly promising, and bore out the sybilline predictions of their late great and
sagacious ruler—Queen Victoria.

'The dear *santissima* woman,' the Pontiff sighed, for he entertained
a sincere, if brackish, enthusiasm for the lady who for so many years
had corresponded with the Holy See under the signature of *the
Countess of Lostwaters.*

'Anglicans . . . ? Heliolaters and sun-worshippers,' she had written
in her most masterful hand, 'and your Holiness may believe us,' she
had added, 'when we say especially our beloved Scotch.' [28]

To return to the novel itself and its construction, it opens in a
flood of impieties and bawdy digressions. The scene is a particularly brilliant one, for it is a state christening attended by the most
elegant of society. To be christened is the aforementioned police
dog, the pet of the Duquessa Dun Eden. Or *is* it a pet? "What—
disquieting doubt,—if it were Her Grace's offspring after all?"
After this genteel suggestion of bestialism, the newly christened
dog and his "parent" indulge in public displays of "incestuous
frolic": a monument is desecrated by the needs of one of them,
the Duquessa is forced into a confessional to repair her rouge
which had been lapped off by her pet, and the whole scene ends
in "stifled yelps" and the "Mauro-Hispanic rafters" of the cathedral ring with confusion.

The doyen of this ecclesiastical world is Cardinal Pirelli who is
of "unusual elegance" and is the possessor of the remains of "perfect good looks." His life is ruled by the Platonic ideal of "balance," which he maintains by combining great piety with an extraordinary private life. He has a mistress for one thing; but, when
she isn't around, he is inclined to dress up "as a cabellero from the
provinces or as a matron (disliking to forgo altogether the military bravoura of a skirt)" and go out onto "the adorable Aveni-
das" in order "to combine philosophy . . . with pleasure." On
one of these occasions he had been pursued by a "persistent officer
who had the effrontery to attempt to molest him"; now he is leading a quieter life. Yet . . . "how entrancing to perch on a bar-
stool, over a glass of old golden sherry."

The cathedral is equally extraordinary: it is famous for its six
dancing boys who enliven the services and provide a diversion for
the pious priests. One of them is known for "the unnecessary un-

dulation of his loins" while another is described as "an oncoming-looking child, with caressing liquid eyes, and a little tongue the color of raspberry cream." The secondary role of these boys is made clear when we overhear "the treble voice" of one of them in an unexpected moment of silence: ". . . frightened me like Father did, when he kissed me in the dark like a lion:—a remark that was greeted by an explosion of coughs."

Because of the precedent-setting christening of the police dog, the cathedral is now beseiged with requests for a similar christening by Amalia Bermudez, an actress and manageress of a theater. Her dog is a Chow who is, literally, full of the Devil, having given birth to a snake which is proof of her evil associations. Amalia succeeds in bringing the secretary of the Chapter around to her way of thinking, so that we find her "considering programmes of music by Rossini and Cimarosa, and the colour of the chasubles which the clergy should wear." The religious tone of the place is further heightened by a forgetful beadle who "had confined by accident a lady in the souterrains of the Cathedral, and only many days later had her bones and a diary, a diary documenting the most delicate phases of solitude and loneliness, *a woman's contribtuion to Science*, come to light; a piece of carelessness that had gone against the old man in his preferment." [29] Firbank tells us all of these things which describe the *ambience* of religious life in Cardinal Pirelli's dominions in a single chapter, another of those panoramic views which include widely diverse characters and allusions united into a composite picture.

The Cardinal's parishioners are chiefly old ladies. The Marchioness of Macarnudo, a Firbankian grotesque, is "crowned with flowers and aigrettes," her fingers "powdered and manicured and encrusted with rings," and her mind is full of her new footman who is "Nothing *classic*—but, oh!" The footman may be beneath her station, but he saves her from something worse:

'I sometimes wish, though, I resembled my sister more, who cares only for amorous, "delicate" men—the Claudes, so to speak. But there it is! And, anyway, dear,' the Marchioness dropped her voice, 'he keeps me from thinking (ah perhaps more than I should) of my little grandson. Imagine, . . . Fifteen, white and vivid rose, and ink-black hair. . . .' And the Marchioness cast a long, pencilled eye towards the world-famous Pietá above her head. 'Queen of Heaven, defend a weak woman from *that!*' she besought.[30]

The Marchioness is "illusion-proof, with a long and undismayed service in Love's House." But she finds her passions very hard to control: "Sometimes she would run out in her car to where the men bathe at Ponte Delgado, and one morning, after a ball, she had been seen standing on the main road to Cadiz in a cabochon tiara, watching the antics of some nude muleteers: *Black as young Indians*—she had described them later." [31] This unabashed sexuality is evident in the "College of the Noble Damsels" as well as everywhere else. We are told of the Abbess who protected the order from a rapacious troop of soldiers: "'I alone,' the Abbess ingenuously states, in relating the affair in her unpublished diary: 'I alone did all I was able to keep them from them, for which they (the scholars) called me "greedy."'" Adding, not without a touch of modern socialism in disdain for titles, that she had preferred 'the staff-officers to the Field-Marshall,' while as to the ensigns, in her estimation, why 'one was worth the lot.'" [32]

The "Poetess Diana Beira Baixa" is one of the most admired women of the city: "Wedded, and proclaiming (*in vers libres*) her lawful love, it was whispered she had written a paean to her husband's '. . . .' beginning *Thou glorious wonder!* which was altogether too conjugal and intimate for recitation in society." [33] Even the Royal Princess, Aurora, has just spent "eight-and-forty hours in bed, and, scandal declared, not alone." Her ancient dog, now blind and "inclined to outlive itself and become a nuisance," dreams of "dark adulteries and dim woods at night."

Many of the paintings on the walls are suggestive or bawdy; we have already noted the picture of the Magdalen "waylaying our Lord," but we read, too, of the "portrait of a Lesbian, with dying fabulous eyes," and of a picture "showing the posterior poudre-derizé of a Saint." A small statue depicts "a pair of hermaphrodites amusing themselves." The pictures, statues, and humans who compose these scenes all combine again into a witch's dance, much like the scene of the Valmouth *fete*, or like one of the canvases of Hieronimus Bosch.

The intensely sexual world of Cardinal Pirelli's parishioners is not very different from the Cardinal's own private life. His mistress and the suggestions of his homosexual activities have already been mentioned. But it is not only in the visible world that Cardinal Pirelli has "experiences." In the visionary and spiritual world his most intensely religious experiences have a distinctly sexual tone. In Chapter VIII, Firbank reaches the apotheosis of all of his grotesque inventiveness; the Cardinal has fled the disgrace that his actions must bring to him and has taken refuge in the decaying Monastery of Desierto, where he plans his *Defense:* "The forsaken splendour of the vast closed cloisters seemed almost to augur the waning of a cult. Likewise the decline of Apollo, Diana. Isis, with the gradual downfall of their temples, had been heralded, in past times, by the dispersal of their priests. It looked as though Mother Church, like Venus or Diana, was making way for the beliefs that should follow . . ." [34]

The Cardinal's life at Desierto is quiet, yet full of simple activity, for he passes his time changing into "dull scarlet crepe, a cobweb dubbed 'summer exile,'" and in pondering the advisability of a henna rinse: "The difficulty was to apply the henna; evenly everywhere; fair play all round; no favouring the right side more than the left, but golden Justice for each grey hair." As the Cardinal's mind wanders in this way, he is filled with the contemplative spirit, which would seem to remove him from the worldliness of sex; but the chapter concludes with a vision, which is one of the most extraordinary scenes in all of Firbank's extraordinary work:

Sometimes, after the fifth or sixth bumper [of liquor] the great Theresa herself would flit in from the garden. Long had her radiant spirit 'walked' the Desierto, seeking, it was supposed, a lost sheet of the manuscript of her *Way of Perfection.* It may have been following on the seventh or even the eighth bumper that the Primate remarked he was not alone.

She was standing by the window in the fluttered moonshine, holding a knot of whitish heliotropes.

'Mother?'

Saint John of the Cross could scarcely have pronounced the name with more wistful ecstasy.

Worn and ill, though sublime in laughter, exquisite in tenderness she came towards him.

'. . . Child?'

'Teach me, oh, teach me, dear Mother, the Way of Perfection.' [35]

The distinctly sexual overtones of the scene, the mixture of drunkenness and divine vision, the hint of sadism in the "knot of whitish heliotropes" with which one imagines Pirelli will shortly be whipped, and the description of St. Theresa of Avilla as "sublime in laughter" all show Firbank at his most impious.

The novel concludes with another remarkable scene. The Cardinal is preparing to flee Spain, but too many bumpers have made it difficult for him to sleep during his last night at home. "Looking fresh as a rose, and incredibly juvenile in his pyjamas of silver-grey and scarlet," he ponders over the memory of one of the boys who has assisted him in a service. The boy had missed all the responses because he had been chasing mice about the cathedral when he should have been attending to the Cardinal. For this the Cardinal has locked him in the cathedral to spend the night alone with the mice. Now the Cardinal, who regrets his cruelty, goes to release the boy from his imprisonment, but not entirely, because he is sorry for having put the boy into a situation in which he might be frightened of the dark. He thinks of the boy as "Don Wilful," "Don Bright-eyes," "Jewel-boy," or "Chicklet"— among several other things. "Setting a mitre like a wondrous mustard-pot upon his head," and feeling "quite rompish," the Cardinal goes to the cathedral:

> It was a night like most.
> Uranus, Venus, Saturn showed overhead their wonted lights, while in the sun-weary cloisters, brightly blue-drenched by the moon, the oleanders in all their wonder—(how swiftly fleeting is terrestrial life) —were over, and the bougainvillaeas reigned instead.
> .   .   .   .
> Two ominous owls answered one another across the troubled garden.[36]

The setting is both Romantic and Gothic:

Someone is following the Cardinal, though we don't find out until nearly two pages later that it is the spying Madame Poco rather than some spirit or a personification of the Cardinal's "conscience":

> Grasping a Bishop's stave, remotely shepherdessy, his Eminence opened softly the door.
> Olé, the Styx!
> Lit by Uranus, Venus and Saturn only, the consummate tapestries on the stairs recording the Annunciation, Conception, Nativity, Presentation, Visitation, Purification and Ascension of the Virgin made welcome milestones. . . . On a turn of the stair by the 'Conception,' a sensitive panel, chiefly white, he had the impression of a wavering shadow, as of someone's following closely behind.[37]

Inside the cathedral, the scene reaches its climax. The light now is nothing more than "the forked fugitive lightning through the triple titanic windows of the chancel." The Cardinal moves slowly through the limbo-like gloom, thinking now and then of the River Styx which, unbeknownst to him, he will soon be crossing. He passes through the chapels of the cathedral and goes down a "spectral aisle"; and then Firbank interrupts the Gothic mood to describe the "chapel of the Magdalen": "Besides the triumphal monument of the beloved of Philip II, the happy (though, perhaps, not the happiest) achievement of Jacinto Bisquert, there were also mural tablets to the Duchesses of Pampeluna (*née* Mattosinhos), Polonio (*née* Charona), and Sarmento (*née* Tizzi-Azza), while the urn and ashes of the Marchioness of Orcasitas (*née* Ivy Harris) were to be found here too, far from the race and turmoil of her native New York." [38]

The Cardinal finally discovers the boy, "Witching as Eros, in his loose-flowing alb, it seemed profane to wake him!"— "'. . . And lead us not into temptation,' the Primate murmured stopping to gaze on him." The Cardinal decides that he will adopt the boy and send him to Oxford, "and perhaps (by some bombshell codicil) make him his heir." He contemplates giving him his Velasquez and his collection of Venetian glass. The lightning and a pinch from the Cardinal awake the boy, who leaps up among the urns and friezes which decorate the cathedral. The Cardinal demands obedience from the boy; but the youth, too wily for him, remains just out of reach. The cathedral nave seems "a place full of strange suggestion . . . intersecting avenues of pillared arches, upbearing waving banners, seemed to beckon towards the Infinite."

The eerie chase continues as old Madame Poco observes from behind the silent statues. The "Chicklet" is an opportunist, and suggests that he will stop running for a price:

'You'd do the handsome by me, sir; you'd not be mean?'
'Eh? . . .'
'The Fathers only give us texts; you'd be surprised, your Greatness at the stinginess of some!'
'. . . ?'
'You'd run to something better, sir; you'd give me something more substantial?' [39]

The boy's demands are a grotesque parody of every maiden's pathetic request for her lover to "do the right thing" by her in Victorian novels.

The mad scene is full of flickering lights and shadows, of ghostly presences and architectural magnificence:

Up and down, in and out, round and round 'the Virgin,' over the worn tombed paving, through Saint Joseph, beneath the cobweb banners from Barocco to purest Moorish, by early Philip, back to Turân-Shâh —'Don't exasperate me, boy'—along the raised tribunes of the choristers and the echoing coro—the great fane (after all) was nothing but the cage; God's cage; the cage; the cage of God! . . .

Through the chancel windows the day was newly breaking as the oleanders will in spring.

Dispossessed of everything but his fabulous mitre, the Primate was nude and elementary now as Adam himself.[40]

This scene concludes with the escape of "Don Temptation," and the naked Cardinal is alone in the church: "He had dropped before a painting of old Dominic Theotocópuli, the Greek, showing the splendour of Christ's martyrdom." The old woman comes out of the shadows to look at the dead Cardinal:

Now that the ache of life, with its fevers, passions, doubts, its routine, vulgarity, and boredom, was over, his serene, unclouded face was a marvelment to behold. Very great distinction and sweetness was visible there, together with much nobility, and love, all magnified and commingled.

'*Adios*, Don Alvaro of my heart,' she sighed, turning away towards the little garden door ajar.

Through the triple window of the chancel the sky was clear and blue—a blue like the blue of lapins. Above him stirred the windblown banners in the Nave.[41]

It would be possible to sentimentalize the Cardinal's death. It is obvious that, as Firbank mocked him, he also admired him; and it is clear that though he "sins," Firbank wants us to believe that there is nobility, distinction, and sweetness in the face of his dead hero. It is best to take the Cardinal at Firbank's appraisal which will lead the reader to finish the novel with a sense of its poignancy. The Cardinal's story is bittersweet, and he is destroyed not only by lust but by the cupidity of the "Chicklet" as well. This final scene of the novel is, stylistically, as fine as anything written during the present century. We wonder if the Cardinal's story would be better known and more widely admired if the "Chicklet" had been a girl—but, of course, the story would then not have been Firbank's; for it would have been only a story of simple lust without the innate absurdities and grotesqueness of the Cardinal's position. This novel is Firbank's most ironic one.

CHAPTER 5

Bits and Pieces

I N 1963 a collection of miscellaneous pieces by Firbank was published under the title of *The New Rythum and Other Pieces*. The volume contains, in addition to the title piece (an incomplete novel), *A Study in Temperament, Lady Appledore's Mesalliance*, "A Miscellany of Short Passages from Unpublished Writings," and a "Short Inventory of Papers found at Romanld Firbank's death." Though none of his work in the volume is first rate, the collection is of the greatest interest; for *A Study in Temperament* and *Lady Appledore's Mesalliance* both come from Firbank's earliest period; and *The New Rythum*, even in its present, incomplete condition, shows the late, mature artist at work.

I   *The Notebook Pages and the Novel*

The cover of *The New Rythum and Other Pieces* reproduces, in facsimile, two pages from the notebook which Firbank was keeping for his new novel; these are worth close attention. Firbank, literally, jammed his notebook with ideas for dialogue, with suggestions for the names of characters, and with fragments of lavish description. Apparently, he would dip into a notebook when in need of a *bon mot* and search for a suitable one. Even though the phrases seem to be put down helter-skelter, we can see that Firbank revised them even while they were in the notebooks. For example: "Mrs. Mandarin Dove—a Sensulist" obviously troubled him. Going back over it, he dropped the "a" and corrected the spelling, so that we get "Mrs. Mandarin Dove—Sensualist." This change is, obviously, not much of a one; and it is no improvement. The next try was "Mrs. Mandarin Dove—The supreme Sensualist" which is an improvement but which is refined even more to "Mrs. Mandarin Dove—a faded Sensualist." She has gone through a Firbankian change from a simple, sensual woman to a woman whose sensuality is, itself, on the wane.

Around this simple phrase are scribbled a number of additional hints about her personality: "hovering about Cath[olicism];" "adores clergymen—The Engl[ish]"; "corresponds with the Bishop"; "an admiration for Cardinal Wiseman." And there are several other apparently irrelevant matters such as "*Tout of the Y.M.C.A.*"; "their homes Vicarage—life"; some suggestions for names, "Partridge" and "Dr. Loader Needelman." There are also tiny phrases, written in Firbank's delicate, slanting hand, such as "had been autre [perhaps outré]"; some references to flower bulbs; a "Prairie Orchid"; the pronunciation of Virginia ("pronounced it Vir-*ginia*"); and a few words which are indecipherable.

All of these bits and pieces are crowded into a very few square inches, apparently without any important order or frame of reference except the original name, "Mrs. Mandarin Dove." It is plain from evidence in several of the later novels that Firbank, whether consciously or not, employed the device of the associative flow; one idea leads to another without the complicated machinery of traditional syntax. These notebook pages show, therefore, how Firbank's mind worked. His imagination was boundless, and he could envision a character or scene with such intensity that a name alone could suffice to define a whole character. As soon as the character had a suitable name, the other bits and pieces of his personality fell into place.

The "Mrs. Mandarin Dove" of the notebook underwent some change before she emerged in *The New Rythum*. For one thing, she became Mrs. Stella Mandarin Dove: "All ardour and zeal, notwithstanding her years, Mrs. Dove was a woman who had been autrefois in the swim. Possessed of a considerable jointure (derived from something supposed to save 'Temper, Time and Money') she now devoted herself to the subduing of the senses, and to a soul-searching correspondence in the style of Christina of Pisa with certain prominent Princes of the Church." [1]

In her house, on East Ninety-first Street—"a frolicsome looking pagan affair"—we see her in conversation with pious churchmen; but it is clear from what follows that she and her friends have been indulging in a whipping session. One guest is still "exalted by her whipping to the last point of gayety." Obviously, though Firbank doesn't use the phrase in the manuscript, Mrs. Mandarin Dove is a faded sensualist; for her "frail cheeks [are] lashed with

paint." The notebook provided, therefore, the image for the creation of a typical Firbankian character, although the specific image
wasn't used in the book.

Several notebook phrases do occur in the novel *The New
Rythum* without any intermediate revision, but these are largely
bits of dialogue, rather than descriptive phrases. Occasionally, a
change is very slight, as "Dr. Loader Needleman's" transformation
into Sir Leonard Needleman; in this case, the first name underwent a rearrangement of letters (and, obviously, a minor addition); and the man rose in social class. The name didn't inspire
Firbank very much, however, for Sir Leonard is described in the
novel as merely being in search of an heiress.

The usual vices, in addition to the whippings already noted, are
very much in evidence. The heroine of the book is having an affair
of sorts with the "Winner of the All America Beauty Prize," Miss
Dreadfuline Hancock of Bloody Brook, Massachusetts; and Bertie
Waldorf, an effeminate young scholar who has compiled a *Glory-
book of Complaisant Husbands,* is planning an assault upon "a
negro lad, in the fruit-picking line, of whom he had some slight
previous acquaintance."

The "rythum," which is new, is that of America. Firbank was
intrigued by the *thought* of New York, although he never visited
it. He pictured New York as a place where everything moved very
fast, where people spoke in peculiar ways, where all of the races
and nationalities of the world combined into a colorful melange—
his vision of America is, in other words, the classic but trite vision
of the country. There are major variations, however, from the normal cliché vision; for opportunity in America is, in *The New
Rythum,* very much like libertinism; the melting pot contains a
very weird mixture indeed; and the speed of American life is positively fantastic. When Firbank attempts to reproduce American
speech, he is inaccurate; but, since exaggeration was always part
of his technique, the exaggerations of American slang and local-
isms are not too far out of line. The difference lies in the fact that
the characters in the earlier novels were upper-class people who
were largely European, and they *sound* it, even when they say
absurd things. Firbank has the Massachusetts Beauty Queen explain the high number of her illegitimate brothers and sisters by
explaining, "Dada, you see, he was inclined to be a baby-making

man." While the idiom may be "American," it is not Massachusetts.

Doubtlessly, Firbank's error arose from the fact that he'd never heard "real" American spoken at any great length, and so he relied upon a "dictionary of American slang and colloquialisms, anticipating a 'sore need of a few really racy words—expressions of the *soil.*'" [2] Whatever dictionary was used,[3] it didn't help Firbank to catch the American idiom with any accuracy; instead, he picked some eccentric phrases or expressions used by Americans, and he simply overused them in his novel. His error is no worse than that of ill-informed Americans who presume that every Englishman's speech is going to be peppered with "Jolly good!" or "Righto!" The results in Firbank's case are funny, however; and they tend to make his characters more grotesque than they would be if they spoke "normal" American English.

American "types" abound in *The New Rythum*. Mrs. Rosemerchant ("née Catherine Cornabilt") is a burlesque of the American society woman with much money and no taste. Most of her time is spent in reading the lurid journals which depict the low life of high society, but she is proud of her "Cornabilt nose." Mrs. Otto Van Cotton is an extraordinarily vulgar woman whose new wealth is used to court the artistic circles of New York and to support the "Ada Beamish Maternity Home," and she has achieved the pinnacle of success by marrying her daughter to a Duke. She is "a striking example of a well-ordered mind in a well-ordered body, the four orbs of her figure being proportioned equally—before and behind." Her home on Fifth Avenue is architecturally like a French chateau, but it has the tasteless external addition of "a couple of smiling Sphinxes, bearing a monogram and the device: *Take Nature as it comes.*" Within, the house contains the riches of the rapacious collector, including a Raphael "madonna with a hoe" which is "an exquisite variation of La Belle Jardinière in the Paris Louvre." Her husband, proud of his collection, likes to invite people to see his sculpture collection with the expansive invitation to "Come and see our boys and girls in stone!" Much of the story revolves around the arrival of the Duchess of Valdivia (née Van Cotton) with a new treasure, a Hercules by Praxiteles which is "Fearsome of buttocks" and "broad of breast."

In *Prancing Nigger*, the Mouth family's Negro dialect was a logical part of the West Indian *milieu;* but in *The New Rythum* Firbank's use of Negro dialect is less fortunate. Mrs. Rosemerchant's page, Co-Co, for example, who is waiting to meet a friend named Posthumus from Harlem "before the public comfort station by Central Park," speaks these words: "Sho', a Child's Diary, or de door ob a church make a more select meetin'-place dan de one Posthumus gib me fo' now." All of the Negroes in this novel speak in this manner, and the notes appended to the book show that Firbank planned to use other phrases such as "fond ob feddehs," "way down Souf," and "a Flower it give a finishment so nice."

A startling view of Firbank's view of "the American way of life" is furnished by the response of two girls when they are addressed by a "big bodied darkie boy" and reply heatedly, "Young man: I guess you're asking to get lynched."

The arrival of the Praxiteles is the high point of the novel:

A brief causerie upon the art of Praxiteles, as contrasted with modern American tendencies and ideals brought the unveiling of the masterpiece to an issue.
'Oh!'
With its look of Nick Tickell, the boxer, there was an exclamation of surprise.
It was Nick; Nick to the very life; without his breeches.[4]

The directors of the Corcoran Gallery in Washington and the Metropolitan in New York both proclaim the statue to be "Stupendous." The "Star Spangled Banner" is sung, the Salvation Army band appears and plays "Mary of Minnesota," and the bored customs officials complete their records:

'Fingers five by three, phallus ten by eight; restored . . .'
. . . .
'They were masterful chaps in them days; eh mates?' a wharf-watchman dormitively observed.
'Abdomen slightly discoloured:' absorbed in statistics the agent deafly pursued.
'Not exactly one of your mortal sort from the look of 'im!'
'Posterior—chipped in two places.'
'Wasn't the old boy a lover of Helen of Troy?' [5]

The city of New York undergoes a most remarkable change from reality: a glamorous place, it is full of trees and spacious avenues; and it bears, therefore, little resemblance to the real New York of the 1920's. Mrs. Rosemerchant lives at 2 Riverside Drive in an attempt to make the Hudson fashionable, when, in fact, Riverside Drive has been a "fashionable" address for many, many years. Grand Central, which Firbank calls "the Central Terminus," is a place of great glamor where "ring-eyed travellers from the violet South" come to the city obsessed with thoughts of Astor, Belasco, and the Criterion. The Croton Reservoir shimmers in the early dusk like "the costliest Tiffany tiara, set in the emerald meadows," while the night air of New York is "mystic oxygen" and the sky above the city is "like the darkest of Cinerarias."

Broadway, at night, is "all poetized": the buildings tower "into the stardust suggesting white shadowy forms endeavouring (vainly) to escape from earth." On a long "tree-shaded Avenue" stands the Convent of Joseph of Arimathea where the nuns are "dreaming of boy saints, mystic marriages and martyrdoms in China and elsewhere." Firbank created another Pisuerga, but it is little wonder that New York is turned into a beautiful and fantastic city, for Firbank began *The New Rythum* in Cairo where he "set up a parasol and 'a little French writing table' in the desert every morning, and "pictured the American scene in a mirage. . . . So beautiful and poetic it seems some times . . . I begin to love it—especially Harlem." [6]

Firbank opened his new novel with a description of New York being caressed by "Zephyr and Flora" on a "pink and elusive evening towards the break of Easter." Easter is rarely a time of pink and elusive evenings in New York; more often, the last remnants of winter chill the paraders on Fifth Avenue. But, of course, this is a fantasy world, "beautiful and poetic" in Firbank's imagination, But all of this leads nowhere in the novel's unfinished condition. An extract from the notebooks gives a hint about the proposed completion of the work. There were to be chapters set in Newport and Palm Beach where there was to be a scene between Mr. and Mrs. Rosemerchant and "Heliodora" (he probably meant Dreadfuline Hancock), with Mr. Rosemerchant demanding his "Conjugal prerogatives," being refused, and finally coming back "in the mood to do anything—even get into bed between them!" [7]

This chapter Firbank wished to make "poetic lyric fantastic anything" (the lack of punctuation is his style), and then to conclude the novel with a finale in which we discover that Mrs. Rose-

merchant and her "young friend" have disappeared: "Rumours
from time to time reached New York that they had been seen
together in Paris restaurants or in Egypt. While some believed
they were living together in the mountains of Nirvana. . . .
Many, and particularly Mr. Rosemerchant's friends, believed
that he had quietly murdered them." [8]

The notebooks give tantalizing hints of other things which
would appear, such as "Theories on Twilight sleep" and, possibly,
a scene in Luna Park. But only the suggestions are there, and it is
pointless to pursue them.

II A Play

We have noted repeatedly that Firbank's writing is often "theatrical"; that is, he sets up scenes which follow one another with
rapidity and in which characters usually "speak" a part, just as
they might in a play. We've also noted that the technique is often
closer to that of the cinema than that of the stage. The costumes
and "sets" in the novels are also more cinematic than theatrical;
for they are like those we used to see in wildly extravagant musical comedies.

Firbank intended to give up ordinary fiction after *Valmouth*
and to switch to the writing of plays. It is clear that he had always
been interested in the theater; for, while at Oxford he had enjoyed
attending the rehearsals of undergraduate productions; and his
earlier, young heroines long for a life on the stage (like Sarah
Sinquier in *Caprice*) or else think of themselves as playing a
"role" in ordinary life (like the heroine of *The Artificial Princess*).
The theater was the only place in the "real" tangible world in
which fantasy can actually exist; therefore, it is not at all surprising that Firbank, who always sought to escape reality, should
have wanted to write for the stage. Both Dickens and Henry
James shared this desire; and both of them, like Firbank, never
had any success with the medium in which they so wished to
shine. Perhaps, in all three cases, their frustration led them to escape into the world of their novels which gave us, in all three
cases, some of each man's best work. Indeed, Firbank's last three
complete novels all date from the time when it was obvious that
his play *The Princess Zoubaroff* was not going to make his fortune
nor enhance his reputation. Ironically, the play was never produced in his own lifetime; and it is perhaps even more ironic that

the novels—as in the case of Henry James—have been the source of several "adaptations" into theatrical pieces.[9]

As a play, *The Princess Zoubaroff* is a failure. Written in three acts and fifty-one "scenes," Firbank indicates a new scene every time a character enters or exits. Fifty-one scenes clearly indicates that the play has a lot of coming and going, and it also has a lot of plot. Briefly told, it is the story of two young couples, Adrian and Nadine Sheil-Meyer and Eric and Enid Tresilian, whose marriages disintegrate in a typically absurd Firbankian way. Eric and Enid are on their honeymoon *chez* Sheil-Meyer in Florence, but the distractions of "society" serve to separate them. Adrian and Eric simply disappear and are not heard of until the closing six scenes (except, that is, in passing references to them) when they return to Florence looking "amazingly fit" and having benefitted from their departure to the point where they look "much younger."

While the men have been away, their wives have entered a convent (though Nadine has borne a child) under the influence of the Princess Zoubaroff, who is described as "a vaguely 'sinister-looking' woman" of about thirty-five. The age of the Princess is of some significance, for it helps us to date the period in which Firbank sets the play. The Princess says that she has been admired by Ingres who "quite worshipped" her little fingers. Since Ingres died in 1867, and assuming that the "knew" her when she was at least an adolescent, the time of the play is somewhere in the 1880's; certainly, it is no later than the 1890's even if we conclude that the Princess is really older than the thirty-five she appears to be, or that Ingres appreciated her as a small child.

The Florence of *The Princess Zoubaroff* bears no relation to any Florence, real or imagined. Almost the entire cast is composed of people who either *are* English, or are vaguely international. Only one Italian appears, a young servant Angelo who is a parody of the parody of an Italian. He is amoral; says things like "Ah, Mamma Mia!"; and expresses a desire to go to America where dollars are obtainable. There are passing references made to churches in the city, to squares, or to the Arno; but this Florence has nothing to do with the typical tourist's idea of the seat of the Italian Renaissance; it is more what he imagines the English colony in Florence to have been like during the residence of the Robert Brownings, with, of course, the addition of Firbankian grotesques who would probably not have been welcome at their Casa Guidi.

The Princess Zoubaroff is, as I say, a bad play—and for much the same reasons that make Firbank's fiction fine. Where Firbank uses the technique of overheard bits of conversation to such effect in the novels, the same technique does not work in the one scene in which it is employed in the play (Act I, Scene XIV). First of all, Firbank uses a much larger cast of characters in most of the novels, and it is usually not important whether or not most of those characters really contribute anything other than overheard conversation. In the novels it is best to imagine ourselves in the conversation scenes as on a balcony, unseen and unimagined— that, in fact, is one of the chief sources of pleasure to us who read the novels. When reading the play, we must deliberately suspend our disbelief and in our mind's eye we must imagine ourselves in the audience with the characters arranged on a stage. Therefore, when we "overhear" parts of different conversations in a scene, we know that the other characters must deliberately pause and allow the bit to be overheard. What seems, in short, to be the most natural thing in the world in the novels seems contrived and laborious in the play.

Firbank labors against another handicap in writing his play: his seemingly uncontrollable desire to describe in detail the clothing his characters wear, the tone of voice in which they speak, and the settings in which they move. When these details are given as stage directions, rather than as part of the unnatural-natural order of things, they lose much of their charm and wit. Like Shaw, Firbank puts much more in his play than could ever meet the eyes or ears of an audience in a theater.

The final and perhaps most serious difficulty with *The Princess Zoubaroff* is that none of the characters is really appealing. We do not expect to "identify" with a Firbank character even in a novel; but, when those characters are made real only by our own imagination, it is possible for us to add the touches which make Lionel Limpness or Sarah Sinquier, for example, appealing in their peculiar ways. As characters in a real play, they seem simply querulous or vaguely repellent.

The reader who seriously desires to "place" *The Princess Zoubaroff* in a literary tradition will have a difficult time doing so. Some critics have compared the play with Congreve's *Way of the World* and have found it to be in the tradition of the "comedy of manners." [10] *The Princess Zoubaroff* is in this school in a peripheral way in that it does deal with the war between the sexes and with the customs of a highly civilized society, but to place the work securely among the comedies of manners is to lose sight of what we know of Firbank's other work. While he is often satirical and is an acute observer of society's fancies, most of his characters and stories go far beyond the realm of the real world and become the inhabitants of Firbank's own mad one. We do not see the story of St. Laura de Nazianzi, for instance, as merely a satire of the life of a saint. Nor should we regard *The Princess Zoubaroff* as a dramatic satirical comedy of manners—the play is too absurd.

Perhaps the concept of the "Theater of the Absurd" is a key to Firbank's achievement in this play. Just as the absurdly funny conversations in Ionesco's *Bald Soprano* do not begin or end in any logical way, so the conversations in *The Princess Zoubaroff* tend to have neither beginning nor end. They are definitely not battles of wit (as they are in Congreve, for example), but tend to be conversations in which characters do not really communicate (as they are in Ionesco). Each character in *The Princess Zoubaroff* speaks about *himself* and his own peculiarities or passions with the result that scenes do not fit together and no real progress toward understanding is made. Each character lives in his own absurd world; and, when he speaks about it, it is juxtaposed against another's absurd world with a result similar to that of the work of the contemporary Absurdists.

If we consider *The Princess Zoubaroff* simply as another "work" by Firbank rather than as a play, we will probably find it more enjoyable. The play contains many fine *bons mots*. The Princess, for example, is irritated by mountains because they are never so high as she would like them to be; as a result, she would "like to shake Switzerland." The newly married Enid is persuaded to wear her wedding band in humid Florence only after she has protested that "It's far too hot to wear a ring," and Blanche Negress (who bears a typically Firbankian name) is described admiringly as "a woman of really advanced morals." Sometimes Firbank's wit shows up best in the stage directions where he directs the actor portraying Reggie Quintus to speak "in a voice which is rather like cheap scent," while Reggie's appearance is described as alternating "between the demi-dazed and the demi-demure."

There are the usual suggestions of perverted sexuality and of Christianity combined with paganism. Enid has been seen "chasing bats after midnight with a long white rosary." The Princess, though she has been married six times, clearly has plans for the postulants in her nunnery who are very worldly. Reggie has millionaire American friends (male) who are unusually attached to him, and he is being kept currently by Lord Orkish whose pastimes include watching the boys "bathing without false modesty of *any* kind" in the Arno. Blanche Negress (who wears a man's cravat in one scene) is the authoress of *Lesbia, or Would He Understand;* and Eric and Adrian flourish in each other's company far more than they do in the company of their wives.

It is easy to see why—aside from the subject of homosexuality—the play was not produced in Firbank's lifetime. Since the public would not accept the fine novels which he produced, it is not surprising that he found no producer willing to present his rather weak play.

III *Youthful Imitation*

Firbank's first book contained *Odette* and *A Study in Temperament*. It was published, at the author's expense, in June, 1905; and it created not a ripple of interest. Firbank (who was still known as "Arthur" rather than as "Ronald") was only nineteen at the time and very much interested in anything *fin de siècle*. The *femme fatale* who figures in so much of the literature of that period appears in *A Study in Temperament:* Lady Agnes Charters is not a very terrifying woman, but she has the appearance and manner of a *femme fatale;* she is dressed in "a long, clinging gown that coiled about her like a dusky snake; her white hands, covered in jewels, shone like glow-worms in the twilight." This description is reminiscent of some of the pictures of Sarah Bernhardt which portray her in snaky-looking dresses and which emphasize the pallor of her complexion.

In Bernhardt we see that combination of the Sphinx-like stare of disdain coupled with the suggestion of smoldering passion that characterizes the *femme fatale;* and, visually, Lady Charters is in this tradition. Actually, she is more like one of the witty heroines of a play by Oscar Wilde; like them, she controls her men through the sheer power of her strong personality rather than through any mystical ability to seduce their minds. Lady Charters only *looks* like a *femme fatale*, but she is fashionable enough to have a lover who is impetuous and who tries to persuade her to go away with him, which would not be very difficult because her husband is rarely at home. "But then," Firbank adds, in a Wildean aside, "there is something so very early Victorian in seeing one's husband, except, of course, sometimes at meals."

In 1905 Firbank's interest in Wilde was strong enough for him to be collecting first editions of his works. Wilde's influence is evident in *A Study in Temperament* in more ways than one might suspect; for Firbank actually lifts, either consciously or unconsciously, an Oscarism from *The Importance of Being Earnest*. In Act III of Wilde's play, the strong-willed Lady Bracknell sums up the faults of her era by saying, "The two weak points in our age are its want of principle and its want of profile." [11] In *A Study in Temperament,* the strong-willed poetess, Hester Q. Tail, sums up the faults of *her* age with the remark that "modern life is only remarkable for its want of profile and its lack of manners." It is impossible to imagine that Firbank did not know of Lady Bracknall's remark, and he was obviously so delighted by Wilde's Victorian lady that some of her words came out of the mouth of one of his own characters. One additional but minor illustration serves to show how much Wilde's work seems to have been in Firbank's mind as he wrote. Hester Tail offers her advice about the best way to succeed in society: "To be artificial, and to be a little more improbable and impossible than one's neighbor, is to be a perfect success!" Wilde, who was the high priest of artificiality, had obviously found a disciple in Firbank. But we must not forget that Firbank was still very young, and obviously susceptible to the influence of a flamboyant figure like Wilde. It is significant to remember Wilde's strong influence at this early point in Firbank's work only so that we may see how truly original Firbank's later work is.

There is no real plot in *A Study in Temperament.* Lady Charters cannot decide whether to run away with Lord Sevenoaks or to dye her hair red—two acts which appear of equal importance to her. She is, in her own words, *"horribly* bored"; she is occasionally moody and capricious. Her sister in law, Mrs. Corba (whose name suggests another snaky *femme fatale*) is equally bored; but her life is made rather squalid by the fact that she is getting fat and must, consequently, pretend always to be in mourning so that the dark colors will hide her broadening figure. Lobelia Corba, niece of Lady Charters, is also a sad case; she has no profile, and life is very difficult for her because of this lack.

Thus, essentially dreary people are the subjects of Firbank's little story; but the dreariness of their minds and their lack of imagination are alleviated by Firbank's own vivid imagination. By the use of clever language and by the addition of neat turns of phrase, Firbank brightens a story which is always trivial and which, in every way, would be dull and trying in the hands of a writer less "clever" than he.

The ennui and "decadence" of Lady Charters and her friends show them to be closely related to the whole movement of the "Yellow Nineties." What they lack in imagination and intellectual vigor they can hide behind a façade of tremendous sophistication. Like Wilde's Dorian Gray, they have well-painted façades which are attractive and pleasant; but, behind the outward appearance of sophisticated world-weariness, we can, if we wish to, discover the moral and intellectual decay which hid behind Dorian's façade. The reader first coming to Firbank, however, should leave moralizing to moralizers; for to belabor any Firbank work, especially at a first reading, with such considerations is to destroy its mood and charm.

In this early work, then, one finds Firbank to be derivative and strongly under the influence of late nineteenth-century Decadent writers, especially Oscar Wilde. There are occasional suggestions of the extraordinary wit that is the hallmark of the later works, but they are no more than suggestions. Where Firbank found it possible to sustain many pages of absurdly humorous conversation in the later novels, his talent now seems to flag very quickly in *A Study in Temperament*. Perhaps the title he chose for his novel (actually, it is no more than a longish short story) is indicative of the ambivalence of his feelings at the time. The word "study," with its overtones of seriousness and scholarly earnestness, suggests that Firbank took his heroine seriously but could not help treating her ironically. And he could not help trotting out "naughty" suggestions of mistresses, dyed hair, and emancipated women.

Within a decade, Firbank was to create his world of extraordinary grotesques; in *A Study in Temperament*, his characters are more like members of a turn-of-the-century Jet Set, flashy and only of momentary interest. Firbank was trying to be chic by being "naughty" and by dropping the names of French writers and by suggesting habits and morals which would clash with the standards of Victorian England. This novel suggests the direction in which he will go, but it shows little promise of the spendid achievements of his later career. When he stopped writing to formula (even an unorthodox formula), he developed his own style and subject matter; and he became a creator instead of an imitator.

IV An "Esthetic" Story

"Lady Appledore's Mesalliance" is a not very successful story about a rich young man, Wildred Forrester, who loses his money and is forced to go to work as a gardener on the estate of a wealthy widow, Lady Appledore. An esthete of a classic sort, Wildred's pregardener rooms are filled with tea roses and wisteria, and on the piano stands "an open piece of music by Debussy"; and his last evening as a member of the idle rich class is spent at the opera where he nearly swoons at the music of *Tristan und Isolde.*

Aside from little details like this, and a considerable amount of detail about Wildred's extraordinary good looks, Firbank does little to develop his central character. Good looks, however, seem to be enough; for Lady Appledore is instantly attracted to her new gardener even though he spends most of his day lying among the branches of trees and reading the *Rubaiyat* of Omar Khayyam. He is discovered when his aunt, the Duchess of St. Andrews, visits Lady Appledore for a week-end house party; and, despite her nephew's entreaties, she reveals his identity. Wildred, aquiver with sensitivity, leaves with these unlikely words to his employer: " 'My dear lady,' he said, 'I am sorry to have to leave you. I have been so happy at Wiston, I am afraid I shall never be happy again, unless'—he broke off—'Oh promise to write and tell me all about the herbaceous borders, and whether old Bartholomew secceeds in inventing a grey Geranium! You do not know how much all your news will interest me.' " [12]

There is, perhaps, some irony intended in this remark; but it is so far removed from the genuinely clever ironic wit of the later novels that one would scarcely suspect it to have been written by Firbank. "Lady Appledore's Mesalliance" is not very important

either in the canon of its author's work or as a late work of the
Decadent period. It is chiefly significant in that it, along with
Odette d'Antrevernes, shows the direction which Firbank's work
might have taken. It might have been simply clever but without
real wit, and it might have done little more than record the foibles
of wealthy and attractive people. Perhaps Firbank might have become a very minor Huxley without Huxley's strong interest in pol-
itics and science.

Instead, of course, Firbank moved in a direction very much his
own and one which took him far from the most frequently trav-
elled literary highways of the period before and during the 1920's.
In this early stage, Firbank is genuinely "twentieth century" in
that he was making some attempt to analyze his characters; but
he was not succeeding very well. In the later works, where the
world passes in front of us like a series of colored scenes, each one
somehow seeming to belong where it occurs, analysis of character
is the last thing in Firbank's mind. Observation is the key to the
later works—observation coupled with a vivid imagination; for
Firbank gives us a real world as it is seen in a distorting mirror.
Both *Odette* and "Lady Appledore's Mesalliance" are strongly
reminiscent of Oscar Wilde's short stories, while *A Study in Temperament* shows Wilde's influence too. All of these early works
are derivative; their chief interest lies in the fact that they continued the Decadence into the twentieth century.

V *Childish Fragments*

The rest of Firbank's work in *The New Rythum and Other
Pieces* is either juvenile or extremely fragmentary. Some of these
fragments, such as the excerpts from "A Tragedy in Green" and
from "When Widows Love," Firbank specifically did not want
published. One of the "short passages from unpublished writings"
is, however, a delightful little glimpse of his mind at "the age of
about twelve": "Mrs. Keston put the dog in its basket, tidid her
hair before a mirror, langwidley sat down and calved a chicken.[13]
[*sic*] This little sentence, apparently written in 1898, shows Firbank's interest in the *fin de siècle* style, for the "langwid" lady is
typical of the period. The spelling is not very far from the kind
which he employed in most of his manuscripts—to the great an-
noyance of his editors and typesetters. Another excerpt, this one
from a "Poem in Prose," shows Firbank's continued association

with Decadence as late as 1905; the "Poem" has the French title necessary for such a piece, "Impression d'Automne" (originally published as "Souvenir d'Automne): "Surely at the foot of the trees that they once made green, which now in the misty air rise like skeletons from the sodden earth, the leaves are lying as though in Purgatory, waiting for the wind to scatter them to the North, to the South, to the East, to the West, as ships are scattered on the sea by the storm." [14] This is another piece of pallid and Frenchified imitation as is "Lady Appledore's Mesalliance" which Firbank wrote in 1898.[15]

Only the giddy foolishness of Firbank's spelling during this period gives a hint of the tone of his later novels, and that hint is, of course, only coincidentally given, Yet both of these passages indicate, even at this early date, his concern with the specific detail and the concrete image. Mrs. Keston, "calving" a chicken with such languid grace, is not really very far removed from the leaves lying in Purgatory.

And his youthful heroines have all the trappings of the properly esthetic lady on the verge of Rome:

A beautiful woman in black was standing in the open window, over her left shoulder fell a great feather boa, and in her hands she held a quantity of blue and white violets. She was very thin and looked pale; her face was half hidden under the long black veil that fell from her hat. On the front of her gown was fashioned a large diamond cross; she wore no other jewels.

She crossed the room to where the great silver crucifix stood and all through the long, long night she prayed for him. . . .[16]

The other fragments in *The New Rythum and Other Pieces* are from youthful efforts which Firbank had marked "Not to be published" [17] and do not really concern us. They were not to be published because they were little more than notes and sketches; Firbank took his writing very seriously and would not have appreciated the publication of even this small amount of unpolished work.

CHAPTER 6

Conclusion

THE first, and perhaps flimsiest, reason for discussing Firbank as a serious and significant writer is the fact that he thought of himself in those terms. His personality made human contact painful for him, but he doggedly produced the novels which permit close inspection by the serious student of literature and, equally, the venom of the outraged moralist. A man's estimate of himself is not always a suitable basis for a literary judgment, but Firbank's seriousness about his work (carefully hidden from most of his friends during his lifetime) demands that the student of literature look at the novels with the closeness he would apply to another writer of sounder and even greater reputation.

Happily, we need not go out on a limb if we conclude that Ronald Firbank is, indeed, a major writer of his period, and one, as Edmund Wilson has asserted, who is "likely to become a classic." Though the general tone of most contemporary criticism of Firbank is of the "He's such a 'camp'" sort, there is a growing interest in him as the serious artist that he truly was. He has been the subject of doctoral dissertations, and the subject of a thorough, scholarly bibliography and biography and his books appear on the reading lists of courses in the contemporary novel at major universities. The heavy hand of scholarship may seem to the casual reader to do more harm than good to Firbank's novels, but the fact remains that we may not dismiss him as a dilettante writer whose work bears only cursory study.

Firbank's achievements are these: he created an imaginary world in his best works that is unlike that in any other English-speaking writer's novels. Not only is this fantastic world full of wit and humor (in both the ordinary and the literary senses of the word), but it is one in which we can come upon sudden, illuminating scenes that enlarge our view of the real world. The bizarre old ladies in *Valmouth* or the innocent natives in *Prancing Nigger,* for example, show us that human nature is pretty much of a piece and that the motives of the unsophisticated and naïve are really no different from those of the worldly and the wealthy. Firbank's West Indians are, on the surface, no more real than his great ladies; but in both we can clearly see the common concerns of humanity tricked out in grotesque trappings. Thus, Firbank's imaginative world is a place inhabited by grotesques with whom we are ill-inclined to associate ourselves, yet these characters are vivid enough to make us see the vanities of the world at large.

True satire holds up the vices and follies of humanity to ridicule and contempt; Firbank uses a satiric method to the extent that he records these vices and follies of humanity in a comic way—but he does *not* imply contempt, nor does he insist that his reader be contemptuous of them. For that reason it is not correct to classify him, in the purest sense, as a satirist. Firbank's approach to human vanity is much more humane than that of the true satirist; he *records* sins and errors, but he does not judge—and neither, therefore, does the reader of his works. Because the comedy inherent in human existence is the chief concern of all of Firbank's major work, he is much closer to the Absurdists of our own period than the satirist who has, throughout history, written for didactic purposes.

Stylistically, Firbank's achievement is far greater than any book about his work can show. The chapter excerpted from *Concerning the Eccentricities of Cardinal Pirelli* (in Chapter 4 of this book) should give the reader a hint of the sophistication of his mature technique and style. It is worth bearing in mind that, when that chapter was written, such techniques as the "associative flow" and stream-of-consciousness were still comparatively unknown in England, yet Firbank has achieved these techniques with great success—such success, in fact, that we may have to return to the chapter to reassure ourselves that it is not the simple, forthright prose of the ordinary novelist. We are led along by the old lady's mind through the intricacies of her own past, present and, even, the foreseeable future. This chapter is not an isolated example; but it is one of the best in the novels.

Everyone has noted Firbank's achievements in dialogue—his method of plunging us *in medias res* without a guide to what has gone before. These overheard, thoroughly intimate conversations are generally so well handled that usually no explanation is needed; Firbank relies on suggestiveness in these scenes to such an extent that the reader is unconsciously forced to create the preceding dialogue. He gives us half a dozen bits and pieces and they suggest a whole world; the precision of his overheard dialogues is so great that nothing more is necessary.

When he is dealing with the setting, on the other hand, he is so lavish in his descriptions that the outer, visible world is built from the ground up—the color of the street, the detail of the buildings, and even the smells and sounds that create these lands that never were. The setting is all there; only the people are left to our imagination which has been guided by no more than a sentence ("Mentally, perhaps, she was already three parts glass"), a description of a fantastic gown, or a snippet of conversation. Though these characters are never real, they take on vivid existence in the mind after a few such hints.

A comparison of Firbank's novels with the paintings of Rubens (or any of a number of other Baroque painters) is helpful; in his pictures, Rubens depicts a world full of flow, movement, and vivid color. The canvases are loaded with detail that melts away into a wash of bright paint if we investigate too closely. Against the lavish backgrounds, his people tend to look isolated—they are too pink, too fat, too smiling, too beguiling; but their absurd lushness is not out of place in the swirling, bright movement of the canvases. In the famous series of paintings in the Louvre of Marie de Medici we see the queen amid the allegorical splendors of fawning gods and goddesses (fawning over the mortal queen), and standing stalwartly ready to dispense justice and bounty to her subjects. Everyone knows that these representations of the queen bear no resemblance to historical fact; but the world the paintings create is complete, and the unlikely, earthly woman in the midst of that grandeur and divine chaos takes on a real existence that no list of facts can ever give to her. The "real" human being is recreated in the imaginative world of the artist until she is unidentifiable in the real world, but she is concrete and very real in the imaginative world. Firbank's characters have exactly the same kind of existence.

Firbank took the *fin de siècle* tradition in English (and French) literature and completely remodeled it. His early work is derivative and imitative, and we come across brief passages even in the later novels that awaken the senses to the strong perfumes and the exotic tastes of that tradition. But, well before he was thirty, Firbank had transformed the "shocking" naughtiness of the *fin de siècle* into witty absurdities of his own. It is perfectly easy to dismiss this achievement with the casual observation that Firbank was not writing during the *fin de siècle* and, therefore, naturally broke away from that tradition; but at that point the biographical factor must enter since Firbank consciously led a public life that had as its model the *ennui* and estheticism of the 1890's, and he was a collector of Decadent literature. The influence of that period, so far removed in spirit, if not in time, from his own was very strong. Since almost no one read or admired his novels anyway, there could have been little motivation for breaking away from a tradition that seemed so thoroughly glamorous. Yet, even as he sat in the old Café Royal in London and with the smart Bohemians of Paris, admiring and curious, he saw through the absurdities and grotesqueness of that existence; his eyes saw the scene, his brain recorded it all, and then his imagination transformed it into Firbankland.

Firbank's subject matter is, as I have said, the vanity, vices, and follies of humanity; but this statement requires expansion, for those are the subjects of all significant writers from Homer to the Absurdist dramatists. It would be foolish to assert that Firbank gives new meanings to man's struggle for perfection; he sees, of course, just as all the other writers have, that perfection is unattainable. What sets him off from most of the others is that we can discern no underlying sense of tragedy in man's failure to reach that idealistic good. His characters suffer endless frustrations, yet, for the most part, they stalwartly pursue their ends. St. Laura de Nazianzi, at the end of *The Flower Beneath the Foot*, is covered with her own blood as she gashes her hands on the broken bottletops capping her convent wall, in an attempt to see the marriage procession of her former lover, the Prince. Her frustration is complete, but the scene ends a novel which has as an epigraph her own statement (taken from her "later" sacred writings): "Some girls are born organically good: I wasn't." The bloody scene may be the climax to a worldly life of frustration, but it is the prologue to a life of sainthood. She overcomes her organic lack of goodness to be canonized in the world of Firbank's incredible saints.

This lack of the tragic element in the novels serves to dehumanize Firbank's world, and to emphasize the irony in all of the sto-

ries. Irony is so central to Firbank's novels that it controls every
scene in the mature work. It is this ironic element which keeps
us from identifying with the characters, and it is the element
which also makes the novels "camp." It is, at the same time, the
element which may support the critic's claim that Firbank will
become a classic. His characters are derived from all of human
experience, but the essentially tragic nature of human experience
is reduced to comedy; death is foolish and provides a time for
the elaborate costuming of the living who will attend the funeral.
Frustration is only a momentary problem which will lead to
sainthood. Lust destroys, but the cardinal dies with a beatific
smile on his face. Human problems lose dignity and become silly
incidents in lives full of triviality. The result is not fiction that is
silly or trivial, but stories rich with irony and humor. It is impossible to imagine vanity and folly appearing so innocent in
another writer's work.

The other vices of Firbank's characters range from sexual perversions to heresy, but they are harmless enough in the Firbank
world where everyone shares them. Secret vice and the hypocrisy
which must accompany it are of no importance; for, where vice
and vanity are the way of life, evil ceases to be evil *per se*.

Firbank is a classic, a writer whose chief works are of genuine
literary excellence; his contribution to the English novel is a major
one; it is an important addition to the long tradition of the English
comic novel, and it offers to the reader a constantly diverting view
of humanity unlike that offered by any other novelist. His work is
genuinely original—in content and in technique.

Notes and References

Chapter One

1. Edmund Wilson, "A Revival of Ronald Firbank," *The New Yorker*, XXV (Dec. 10, 1949), p. 127.

2. All quotations from Firbank's work, unless otherwise specifically noted, are taken from the New Directions editions with their permission. These editions are, *The Complete Ronald Firbank* (Norfolk, Conn.: 1961) and *The New Rythum and Other Pieces* (Norfolk, Conn.: 1963).

Novels included in *The Complete Ronald Firbank* are cited as "*Vainglory* [etc.], in *The Complete Ronald Firbank*, p—" in the first reference, and thereafter with the title of the novel alone. The page reference is always to the New Directions edition. Quotations from *The New Rythum and Other Pieces* are always cited as "*The New Rythum*, p—" and the page number again refers to the New Directions edition.

3. He told one acquaintance, "I think nothing of fileing [*sic*] fifty pages down to make a brief, crisp paragraph, or even a row of dots." (v. Miriam J. Benkovitz, "Ronald Firbank in New York," *New York Public Library Bulletin*, LXIII [May, 1959], p. 258, where the letter containing this remark is quoted). While Firbank was doubtlessly exaggerating, the evidence of his notebooks and revisions proves that he labored endlessly to create the effect of casual brilliance.

4. A facsimile reproduction of Firbank's autograph "Preface" for *The Flower Beneath the Foot* (Brentano's), New York, 1924, appears in the first American edition. Again, he is doubtlessly exaggerating for effect, but we may see from his words how his creative processes worked.

5. *The New Rythum*, p. 71.

6. Quoted in *Ronald Firbank: A Memoir* (London: 1930), p. 16. This book contains pieces by I. K. Fletcher, Lord Berners, V. B. Holland, Augustus John, and Osbert Sitwell. References to it hereafter will cite the name of the author of the section quoted, the short title *Memoir* and the page number.

7. Fletcher, *Memoir*, p. 19.

8. *Ibid.*, p. 25.

9. *Ibid.*, p. 22.
10. *Ibid.*, p. 27.
11. The page is reproduced in facsimile facing page 88 in *The New Rythum.*
12. Fletcher, *Memoir*, p. 33.
13. The observation was actually made by A. C. Landsberg, but is quoted by Fletcher in *Memoir*, p. 37.
14. Holland, *Memoir*, p. 107.
15. Fletcher, *Memoir*, p. 44.
16. *Ibid.*, p. 45.
17. Sitwell, *Memoir*, p. 118.
18. Fletcher, *Memoir*, p. 47.
19. Sitwell, *Memoir*, p. 130.
20. Quoted by Fletcher, *Memoir*, p. 67.
21. Lord Berners, *Memoir*, p. 147.
22. *Ibid.*, pp. 147–48.

Chapter Two

1. *Odette*, in *The Complete Ronald Firbank*, p. 20.
2. *Ibid.*
3. *Ibid.*, p. 24.
4. *Ibid.*, p. 25.
5. *Ibid.*
6. *Inclinations*, in *The Complete Ronald Firbank*, p. 285.
7. *Ibid.*, p. 295.
8. *The Artificial Princess*, in *The Complete Ronald Firbank*, p. 28.
9. *Ibid.*, p. 32.
10. For a brief description of Strauss's technique in *Salome*, see Philip Keppler, "Sparkle of Sound," *Opera News*, XXIX (March 13, 1965), pp. 24–25.
11. *The Artificial Princess*, p. 53.
12. *Ibid.*, pp. 51–52.
13. *Ibid.*, pp. 71–72.
14. *Ibid.*, pp. 61–62.
15. *Ibid.*, p. 55.
16. *Ibid.*, p. 62.
17. *Ibid.*, p. 62.
18. Miriam J. Benkovitz, *A Bibliography of Ronald Firbank* (London, 1963), p. 62. Referred to hereafter as *Bibliography.*

Chapter Three

1. Grant Richards, *Author Hunting* (New York: 1934), pp. 248–49.
2. *Ibid.*, p. 250.
3. *Ibid.*, p. 254.

4. Lord Berners, in *Memoir,* p. 146.

5. *Ibid.,* pp. 146–47.

6. Quoted by Fletcher, *Memoir,* p. 60.

7. *Ibid.,* p. 55.

8. Richards, *op. cit.,* p. 250.

9. *Vainglory* in *The Complete Ronald Firbank,* p. 76.

10. W. M. Thackeray, "Codlingsby, by D. Shrewsbury, Esq.," in "Novels by Eminent Hands," *Works,* vol. XVIII (New York: 1911), pp. 22–42.

11. *Vainglory,* p. 80.

12. *Ibid.,* p. 82.

13. *Ibid.,* p. 94.

14. *Ibid.,* p. 92.

15. *Ibid.,* p. 98.

16. *Ibid.,* p. 106.

17. *Ibid.,* p. 173.

18. *Ibid.,* p. 198.

19. *Ibid.,* p. 165.

20. *Caprice* in *The Complete Ronald Firbank,* p. 368.

21. *Ibid.,* pp. 333–34.

22. *Ibid.,* pp. 364–65.

23. *Ibid.,* p. 371.

24. Jocelyn Brooke, *Ronald Firbank* (London: 1951), p. 66.

25. Benkovitz, *Bibliography,* p. 29.

26. *Valmouth,* in *The Complete Ronald Firbank,* p. 463.

27. *Ibid.,* pp. 388–89.

28. *Ibid.,* p. 391.

29. *Ibid.,* p. 416.

30. *Ibid.,* p. 425.

31. *Ibid.,* pp. 402–03.

32. *Ibid.,* p. 406.

33. *Ibid.,* p. 407.

34. *Ibid.,* p. 429.

35. *Ibid.,* p. 440.

36. Benkovitz, *Bibliography,* p. 35.

37. *Ibid.*

38. *Santal,* in *The Complete Ronald Firbank,* p. 486.

39. *Ibid.,* p. 490.

40. *Newsweek,* XLV (March 21, 1955), p. 109.

41. Benkovitz, *Bibliography,* p. 29.

Chapter Four

1. Quoted by Benkovitz, in *Bibliography,* p. 38.

2. *Ibid.,* pp. 37–38.

3. *The Flower Beneath the Foot,* in *The Complete Ronald Firbank,* p. 516.

4. See Note 4, Chapter 1.

5. *The Flower Beneath the Foot,* p. 500.

6. In a letter to his mother (quoted in Benkovitz, *Bibliography,* p. 39) Firbank said that she is "Mrs. Harold Nicolson," who, of course, was not a "Romantic novelist," but Victoria Mary Sackville-West, whose novels do not seem to me to resemble Mrs. Chilleywater's at all.

7. *The Flower Beneath the Foot,* p. 559.

8. *Ibid.,* p. 565.

9. *Ibid.,* p. 536.

10. According to the letter cited in note 6, above, "King Geo." and Queen Glory, the English sovereigns who visit Pisuerga, are modelled upon the English King and Queen (George V and Queen Mary), and Firbank is rather unkind to them; they are extremely dull, and the Queen of Pisuerga is rather ashamed of her newly formed family connection with them. When Firbank wrote about royalty, he never achieved the heights he did when writing about the *nouveau riche* and the upper-middle classes who aspired to higher things.

11. *The Flower Beneath the Foot,* p. 501.

12. *Ibid.,* p. 542.

13. *Ibid.,* p. 505.

14. *Ibid.,* p. 542.

15. Benkovitz, *Bibliography,* p. 39 (where Firbank's letter is quoted).

16. *The Flower Beneath the Foot,* p. 543.

17. *Ibid.,* p. 550.

18. *Ibid.,* p. 553.

19. *Ibid.,* p. 587–88.

20. *Ibid.,* pp. 545–46.

21. *Ibid.,* p. 579.

22. Carl Van Vechten, "Preface" to *Prancing Nigger* (New York, 1924), p. v. Ensuing references to *Prancing Nigger* are from the New Directions edition (see note 2, Chapter 1) and not to the Brentano edition cited here.

23. *Prancing Nigger,* in *The Complete Ronald Firbank,* p. 601.

24. *Ibid.,* p. 637.

25. *Ibid.,* pp. 625–26.

26. *Ibid.,* p. 615.

27. *Concerning the Eccentricities of Cardinal Pirelli,* in *The Complete Ronald Firbank,* pp. 665–69. In ensuing references, the title of this novel will be shortened to *Cardinal Pirelli.*

28. *Ibid.,* p. 658.

29. *Ibid.,* p. 653.

30. *Ibid.*, p. 662.
31. *Ibid.*, pp. 674–75.
32. *Ibid.*, p. 669.
33. *Ibid.*, p. 664.
34. *Ibid.*, p. 679.
35. *Ibid.*, pp. 683–84.
36. *Ibid.*, p. 691.
37. *Ibid.*, p. 692. There is a notable similarity between the scene here and some of the images in T. S. Eliot's "Ash Wednesday," especially II, 96 ff. The similarity can only be a coincidence since "Ash Wednesday" was not published until 1930, unless, of course, Eliot knew *Cardinal Pirelli.*
38. *Ibid.*, p. 693.
39. *Ibid.*, p. 696.
40. *Ibid.*, p. 697.
41. *Ibid.*, pp. 697–98.

Chapter Five

1. *The New Rythum,* p. 106.
2. Quoted by Allan Harris in the "Introduction" to *The New Rythum,* p. 14.
3. H. L. Mencken's *The American Language* had been published in 1921 and republished with extensive revisions in 1923. It may well have been the book used.
4. *The New Rythum,* p. 93.
5. *Ibid.*, pp. 94–95.
6. Benkovitz, *Bibliography,* p. 70.
7. "Extracts from the notebooks," in *The New Rythum and Other Pieces,* p. 108.
8. *Ibid.*, p. 109.
9. For a record of these adaptations, see Benkovitz, *Bibliography,* especially pp. 46–47, item 29.
10. V. Cyril Connolly, *Enemies of Promise,* p. 42, or Edmund Wilson, "A Revival of Ronald Firbank," either in *The New Yorker* (December 10, 1949), p. 129, or the reprint of this essay in *Classics and Commercials.*
11. *A Study in Temperament,* in *The New Rythum,* p. 26.
12. "Lady Appledore's Mésalliance," in *The New Rythum,* p. 64.
13. "A Miscellany of Short Passages from Unpublished Writings," in *The New Rythum,* p. 115.
14. *Ibid.*, p. 116.
15. Miriam J. Benkovitz, "A Chronology of Ronald Firbank," on p. 351 of *Ronald Firbank: Two Novels.* New Directions paperback, ND 128 (New York, 1962).

16. *Ibid.*

17. Benkovitz, *Bibliography,* in which the typescripts are described on pp. 85–91.

Selected Bibliography

PRIMARY SOURCES

1. First Editions

FIRBANK, RONALD. *Odette D'Antrevernes and A Study in Temperament.*
London: E. Mathews, 1905. N.H. This book was published under
the author's full name, Arthur Annesley Ronald Firbank.

Vainglory. London: Grant Richards, 1915.

Inclinations. London: Grant Richards, 1916.

Odette, A Fairy Tale for Weary People. London: Grant Richards, 1916.
"Slightly revised version" of the 1905 edition of *Odette.*

Caprice. London: Grant Richards, 1917.

Valmouth. London: Grant Richards, 1919.

The Princess Zoubaroff. London: Grant Richards, 1920.

Santal. London: Grant Richards, 1921.

The Flower Beneath the Foot. London: Grant Richards, 1923.

Prancing Nigger. New York: Brentano, 1924. (*Sorrow in Sunlight.*
London: Brentano.)

Concerning the Eccentricities of Cardinal Pirelli. London: Grant
Richards, 1926.

The Artificial Princess. London: Duckworth, 1934.

The New Rythum and Other Pieces. London: Duckworth, 1962.

2. Other Editions and Collections

Sorrow in Sunlight. London: Brentano, 1924. Title given to the first
English edition of *Prancing Nigger.*

The Works of Ronald Firbank. 5 vols. London: Duckworth, 1928.

"Rainbow Edition." 8 vols. London: Grant Richards, 1929–30.

"Omnibus Edition." 2 vols. London: Grant Richards, 1949–50. Two
volumes of this edition are entitled *Five Novels* and *Three Novels.*

Extravaganzas. New York: Brentano, 1935. Contains *The Artificial
Princess* and *Concerning the Eccentricities of Cardinal Pirelli.*

The Complete Ronald Firbank. London: Duckworth, and New York:
New Directions, 1961. This edition, the most readily available,
has been used throughout this book, to simplify references.

Two Novels. New York: New Directions, 1962. New Directions paperback (ND 128); contains *The Flower Beneath the Foot* and *Prancing Nigger*.

SECONDARY SOURCES

BENKOVITZ, MIRIAM J. *A Bibliography of Ronald Firbank.* London: Rupert Hart-Davis, 1963 (Soho Bibliographies, no. 16). Thorough, scholarly bibliography of all of Firbank's work published through 1962. In addition to full bibliographical information, there is a wealth of biographical material relevant to the creation and publishing of each work. This book supercedes all other bibliographies and is indispensable to anyone seriously interested in Firbank.

————. "An Early Flemish Painter, by Ronald Firbank." *New York Public Library Bulletin,* LXXII (Dec. 1968).

————. "Notes Toward a Chapter of Biography: Lord Alfred Douglas and Ronald Firbank." *New York Public Library Bulletin,* LXVII (March, 1963), pp. 143–51. Treats the brief friendship of the two men. Firbank admired Douglas as an older, more eminent man; but, as he matured, he liked Douglas less and less.

————. "Ronald Firbank in New York." *New York Public Library Bulletin,* LXIII (May, 1959), 247–59. A useful record of Firbank's friendship (by mail) with Carl Van Vechten who introduced his work in the United States and who was responsible for the publication of *Prancing Nigger* in New York (1924). Some biographical details of interest, and a quotation from a letter saying that Cardinal Pirelli was "inspired" by Ilundain y Esteban, Archbishop of Seville. Firbank never visited the United States, so the title refers to his success in America in a literary sense.

BROOKE, JOCELYN. *Ronald Firbank and John Betjaman.* London: British Council, 1962. Writers and Their Work, No. 153. Slight. The title should not be construed to mean that the two men are compared or dealt with jointly; the British Council has frugally combined the two authors in one volume.

————. *Ronald Firbank.* London: A. Barker, 1951. Brief but sympathetic study of Firbank's work. Concludes that Firbank is both "typical of the nineteen-twenties" and "timeless." Firbank, says Brooke, should be read purely for pleasure.

CONNOLLY, CYRIL. *The Condemned Playground: Essays, 1927–1944.* London: Macmillan, 1945. Connolly was one of Firbank's earliest admirers among the influential critics. The section dealing with Firbank is brief but perceptive. He compares Firbank's style with Mozart's: "That doesn't mean I think he is as good as Mozart, . . . but that in him more than in any contemporary writer I

find that taste. He and the early Eliot seem to me the pure artists
of the 'twenties. . . ." (p. 115).

———. *Enemies of Promise.* Boston: Little, Brown, 1939. A discussion of Firbank as a dandy in the style of the seventeenth century.
Connolly says that Firbank took pains to hide his intellectualism.
He places *The Princess Zoubaroff* in the school of Congreve (42).
"The lesson one can learn from Firbank is that of inconsequence."
". . . it is to Firbank that we owe the conception of dialogue—
not as a setpiece in the texture of the novel, as are the conversations of Wilde and Meredith—but as the fabric itself." (Both
quotes, 45.)

DAVIS, ROBERT MURRAY. "'Hyperaesthesia with Complications': The
World of Ronald Firbank." *Style,* 1968. A good review of Firbank's achievements.

DICKENSON, PATRICK. "A Note on Ronald Firbank." I, 3 *Windmill*
(1946), 26–36. Appreciative essay.

FLETCHER, IFAN KYRLE. *Ronald Firbank: A Memoir.* London: Duckworth, 1930 (and New York: Coward, McCann, 1932). One of
the very few sources of biographical information currently
available. In addition to Fletcher's *Memoir,* the book contains
"Personal Reminiscences" by Lord Berners, V. B. Holland, Augustus John, and Osbert Sitwell (the latter also appears in Sitwell's
Noble Essences [Boston: Little, Brown, 1950] and as an Introduction to the first volume of *Five Novels* in the "Omnibus Edition"). Fletcher's contribution covers all of Firbank's life, while
the others touch upon specific incidents or brief periods of Firbank's life. Much of the biographical material in this book comes
from this *Memoir* which has been cited wherever it was used.

FORSTER, E. M. *Abinger Harvest.* New York: Harcourt, Brace, 1936.
115–21. Forster begins his essay with the metaphorical remark
that it is unwise to "break a butterfly upon a wheel" and then
implies that Firbank is more than a butterfly. This brief essay is
interesting because it is the critical judgment of an important contemporary novelist upon another important, though far less successful (in terms of his fame), modern novelist. Written shortly
after Firbank's death.

JONES, E. "The World of Ronald Firbank." *Nation,* CLXIX (November 26, 1949), 520–21. Jones says that Firbank "is the first novelist to celebrate café society." In his novels, "homosexuals are the
ultimate *chic*" but that there is a "tough core of common sense" in
his fiction. "He is also one of the few Georgian novelists who scrupulously eschewed the dead-end of Realist-cum-Naturist fiction.
Compares Firbank with the Wilde of *Dorian Gray,* Baron Corvo,

and Ivy Compton-Burnett "with the passion left out." His characters stem "from the rich tradition of British eccentricity." "Like
Joyce and Virginia Woolf, he relied on the methods of poetry, the
drama, and impressionist painting." Jones finds the novels "poign-
ant" because of their "sense of mortality." Though this brief
review was intended to be little more than a review, it is full of
insight.

MUIR, PERCIVAL H. "A Bibliography of the First Editions of Books by
Arthur Annesley Ronald Firbank" (Supplement to *Bookman's
Journal*, 3rd Series, XV, 1 (1927). Miss Benkovitz's *Bibliography*
(see above) supersedes this one and makes several corrections
in addition to being more thorough and up-to-date.

"Strange Bird." *Newsweek*, XLV (March 21, 1955). 109–10. Only
a review of *Santal* but interesting because of the anonymous
writer's view of the novel as a "vivid footnote on faith" and as "a
tender Persian miniature." It is also "entirely musical" and evokes
the Moslem world.

NICOLSON, HAROLD. *Some People*. London: Constable, 1927. Character
Gilbert Orme is supposed to be modelled after Firbank's appearance and mannerisms, though not upon his life. Firbank felt some
antipathy for the Nicolsons, though Sir Harold had been at a
party honoring Firbank in Rome in 1923. In *The Flower Beneath
the Foot* (1923) the silly lady novelist, Mrs. Chilleywater, was
supposed to be Mrs. Harold Nicolson, as was the English Ambassadress (see p. 39 of Benkovitz, *Bibliography*, for the letter from
Firbank to his mother which makes this identification).

REDMAN, B. R. "Quintet From a Minor Dream Garden." *Saturday Review of Literature*, XXXIII (February 25, 1950), 17. Redman
says that Firbank's novels have revived because of the collapse
of the Marxian dream. He finds Firbank to be "minor"; his stories,
only "fairy tales."

RICHARDS, GRANT. *Author Hunting*. New York: Coward-McCann,
1934. 248–60. Richards' remarks about Firbank have been cited
in this study at some length. They are of great interest in that
they show the practical mind of the publisher in conflict with the
impractical mind of the artist. Richards relates several anecdotes;
and, though he misjudges Firbank, he makes a sincere attempt to
appreciate him. Almost all of Firbank's novels were first published
by Richards (at Firbank's own expense).

SITWELL, OSBERT. *Noble Essences*. Boston: Little, Brown, 1950. This
contains the essay included in the I. K. Fletcher *Memoir* (see
above).

"More Than Just a Dandy." *Time*, LXXVIII (Nov. 19, 1961), p. 99.
Of interest because it is a popular press view of Firbank. The

anonymous reviewer says that Firbank found that "life is cruel, beautiful and impossible to explain." The review is almost completely sympathetic and admiring.

VAN VECHTEN, CARL. *The Double Dealer.* April, 1922. This article did much toward making Firbank successful in America. Van Vechten said that the books were unsuitable for public libraries and that Firbank was "Aubrey Beardsley in a Rolls-Royce" and "Jean Cocteau at the Savoy." Van Vechen's admiration for Firbank came at a time when he had received only casual praise in England. Van Vechten also arranged for the publication of "A Broken Orchid" (a chapter from *Sorrow in Sunlight* in *The Reviewer* in October, 1923) and the first edition of *Prancing Nigger* (American title, and, therefore, first edition title, of *Sorrow in Sunlight*).

WAUGH, EVELYN. *Life and Letters Today,* II, 10 (1929), 191–96. Early appreciation of Firbank by a major contemporary novelist.

WILSON, EDMUND. "Firbank and Beckford." *New Republic,* XIVIII (September 8, 1926), pp. 70–71. Discussion of the similarities between Firbank and "Vathek" Beckford, and especially their love of elegance and the influence of French literature upon them.

————. "Revival of Ronald Firbank." *New Yorker,* XXV (December 10, 1949), pp. 127–35. Republished in *Classics and Commercials.* Astute, useful summary of Firbank's work; the essay in which Wilson says that Firbank is "one of the finest English writers of his period and one of those most likely to become a classic." He points out the similarity between the personalities of Firbank and Proust; offers a brief biography, though the biographical information is not an addition to that to be found elsewhere; and places Firbank in the English comic tradition of Ben Jonson, Congreve, T. L. Peacock, W. S. Gilbert, and Aldous Huxley.

Wilson finds *The Princess Zoubaroff* to be "an understatement of the same theme that D. H. Lawrence became violent and shrill about: the biologically sinister phenomenon of a slackening of the interest in mating on the part of the privileged classes of Europe." *Cardinal Pirelli* has the most "moral meaning" of the novels and is Firbank's "ideal conception" of what the Catholic religion might be, though the view is "quite heretical but not irresponsible."

The importance of Wilson as a critic, and his intelligent, perceptive appreciation of Firbank make this one of the most important critical essays dealing with him.

Index

147